Trout and Salmon

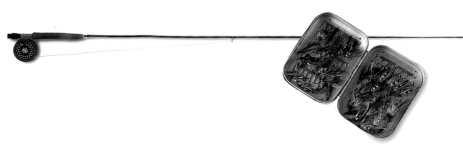

Trout and Salmon

PHOTOGRAPHY BY R. VALENTINE ATKINSON

THE LYONS PRESS

DEDICATION

My grateful thanks go to Susan Rockrise for her generous assistance,
creative vision, and boundless enthusiasm. I will always be thankful for
her love and support which helped make this book possible.

Trout and Salmon
The Greatest Fly Fishing for Trout and Salmon Worldwide

Library of Congress Cataloging-in-Publication Data
Atkinson, R. Valentine.
    Trout & salmon : the greatest Fly Fishing for trout and salmon
    worldwide / photography by R. Val Atkinson. — 1st U.S. ed.
        p.   cm.
    ISBN 1-55821-804-1 (cloth)
    1. Trout fishing.   2. Salmon fishing.   3. Fly fishing.   I. Title.
    II. Title: Trout and salmon.
    SH687.A85   1999
    799.1'757—dc21   98-37525
                                                            CIP

Color reproduction by Colourscan, Singapore
Printed in Hong Kong by Imago Limited

2 4 6 8 9 7 5 3 1
First U.S. Edition published for The Lyons Press,
123 West 18th Street, 6th Floor, New York, New York 10011

Created and designed by Duncan Baird Publishers Ltd
6th Floor, Castle House
75–76 Wells Street, London W1P 3RE

Consultant Editor: Nick Zoll
Managing Designer: Gabriella Le Grazie
Designers: John Grain, Dan Sturges
Managing Editor: Judy Dean
Editor: Kirsty Seymour-Ure
Editorial Assistant: Emma Prunty
Studio photography: David Murray
Commissioned map artwork: Neil Gower
Commissioned artwork: James Prosek
Calligraphy: Susanne Haines

Typeset in 10.5 pt Ehrhardt MT

PUBLISHERS' NOTE
The captions in this book are by R. Valentine Atkinson.
The publishers and the photographer would like to voice their support for the principles of
"catch and release" and all other forms of fishery enhancement and conservation.

Contents

Foreword

What a visual and verbal feast, this second collection of superb photographs by Val Atkinson, with essays by John Gierach, Clive Gammon, Tom McGuane, Brian Clarke, Zane Grey, Roderick Haig-Brown, Ernest Schwiebert, and a small company of other anglers.

The essays seek to capture the physical qualities of the dozen places depicted in this rich book – from the United States to Russia, with sections on Ireland, Canada, Argentina, Chile, New Zealand, Scotland, Norway, and other regions of the world with bright rivers and exceptional trout or salmon fishing. But the prose goes further. In the various voices of the writer-anglers, and through their differing eyes, we meet unforgettable local characters, eat some memorable meals, and experience the suspense and drama of a hundred fishing occasions, from the common to the fully uncommon. Big fish are hooked and caught – or perhaps they are lost; but you can also travel with John Gierach, always the best of company, up a western canyon to its headwaters, where the "fish are eager, slightly stupid, and not large," where you get a strike nearly every time you put a good cast over a rising trout. And from there we're off to big fish again, Tom McGuane's "hard-running ocean-bright fish," a salmon that ends in the net, "a big deep hanging silver arc." Fish are caught because fishermen know not only how to fish but, first, where to find them. Throughout these essays there is the kind of knowledge that must always come before catching is possible. "Salmon hold in its first sixty meters of current," writes Ernest Schwiebert of a Norwegian river. "They lie under swirling currents of sapphire and spume, where the stream wells up silken and smooth, before the river grows shallow over a tail of fine cobble." And between the big fish and the small fish, the portraits of people and rivers, the shrewd knowledge of where the fish are, there is the fishing itself, as wonderfully real and even abrupt as one might want. "Running a fly down Rocky Cast one evening," writes David Profumo, "there was a flash of grey flank and my small Stoat just below the surface was cancelled like a typing error."

Surrounding the words, both illuminating them and forming a world and story – or, rather, many stories – all their own, are Val's photographs. They are the finest of his that I have ever seen. They seem to have grown finer and sharper, closer to some seminal understanding of what all this fuss about trout and salmon, and the ways some of us pursue them, is really about.

There is one photograph of a small headwaters stream, with a man cross-legged, nearly camouflaged, resting and watching. In another, two men peer down from an old stone bridge, as I have done a thousand times, as all fishermen have done and will always do – for a bridge uniquely puts you directly above a river, not to its side, and you can peer down into the mysterious, watery world of our quarry, even as Nick Adams did in the Hemingway story, and see resting or working trout, and marvel at their lithe movements, and learn just a bit more about a world that is not ours. I have learned volumes by staring down into that three-dimensional liquid from bridges: where trout rest, how they hold in the current, the nature of their rise, how they take a nymph, and so much more.

These are simple scenes, not sentimental but poignant to any fisherman. And so are the casts of the fly, with the line frozen in fluid motion; bigger water, in Alaska or Russia, or a small spring creek that is its own world, wherever it happens to flow. There are stunning photographs of anglers probing crystalline waters with expectation in their crouch and stretch, and others of great fish on in big water, fish that are sometimes caught, that look to be ten or twelve pounds' worth of brown trout, or larger salmon, bright silver. I like the seaplane in a vast remote world, approaching its haven, and the disturbed grizzly looking up, whether curious or mad we cannot tell. I like the leaping salmon and the wilderness scenes and some salmon steaks on a grill, with lemon and onion, bright red. I like the always different skies and the many different boats fishermen use and the broad curve of the long rod when a good fish is on. I love the dozens of new waters Val shows us – flat, riffled, raucous, flowing through meadows or over lava beds.

What I love most, I think, is that Val's eye catches the quintessential moments of fly-fishing, those elemental times when everyone who fishes with this kind of equipment becomes part of the same process. I like the fact that his photographs here, in contrast to those in his previous book, are highlighted by being larger, more simple, better able to reveal more of the world they record. They are especially remarkable in their ability to define for us what we all love so much about fly-fishing, especially for trout and salmon, wherever they are found.

Nick Lyons

Introduction

The success of my first book, *Distant Waters*, more than fulfilled a life-long dream: it challenged me to produce this second book that I might share some exciting new fly-fishing destinations with you.

Fly-fishing, photography and travel work very well together – each one complements the others. I've grown up with an insatiable wanderlust – a love of visiting and fishing new places. When I'm not actually traveling I'm often daydreaming about some beautiful new destination with rivers full of trout or salmon. I also love running film through my camera, so that I might have some evidence of this beauty to share with others. My father is a photographer and he helped instill a love of photography in me at an early age. I feel extremely fortunate to have managed to combine these passions over the years into a profession. I love my job.

Friends often ask me how in the world I manage to find time to photograph when I'm out fishing. How can I really do two things at once? The secret is timing. It's simply a question of when you put down the rod and pick up the camera. I always have both at the ready. When out on the stream, I'm looking for good light in a spectacular setting. I'll shoot *action* whenever and wherever it occurs. As I head out in the morning, I carry a backpack which holds my fly-rod as well as my tripod and an assortment of lenses. I can photograph until the sun rises too high for good pictures, warming the water as it climbs: there consequently may be a hatch, and I'll put away the camera and go fishing. The trick is knowing when to do what. I often follow friends and models around waiting for something to happen. When it does and I've taken some good shots, I'll put down the camera and fish awhile myself.

A good example of this special sense of timing occurred this past summer in Ireland, where I was photographing for this book. My fishing companions and I were staying at Stuart Mcteare's fishing lodge on Lough Sheelin, a lovely place known for its big brown trout. Located on an inlet to the lough, the lodge is very conveniently placed right next to Watty's Rock, the best pub in the village.

The mayfly hatch was on and every day we sallied forth to try for one of the "big boys." We fished early, we fished late, we fished hard in the rain – but we couldn't seem to catch a good fish for the camera. (This happens to me a lot.) On our last outing, just at twilight, I was standing on the shore, talking softly with Dennis, our guide, in the gathering gloom. My friends were casting their way up the shoreline when suddenly Dennis stopped in mid-sentence and pointed right beside our beached boat – a fish had just taken a skittering caddis, or murrough, as they are known in Ireland. "Take the spare rod in the boat and have a go at him, Val," said Dennis in his wonderful Irish accent.

I put down my camera, picked up the rod, and put a freshly tied Murrough over the fish – my very first cast of the entire trip. Up he came and engulfed that fly. I landed a beautiful five-and-a-half-pound Lough Sheelin brown trout on one cast. Can you imagine the heat I took that night at Watty's Rock? Rounds of Guinness for everyone!

So that's what I mean about timing. It's everything in life.

I would like to thank the following friends for their continued support:
Alex Mitchell, Nick Zoll, Duncan Baird, the design and editorial teams at Duncan Baird Publishers, Frontiers International Travel, Susan Rockrise, Louise Grimsley, Nick Lyons, and all my friends who have been models along the way – thank you, you're a part of all this.

Here's to truth, adventure, and passion in fly-fishing, travel, and life!

R. Valentine Atkinson
September 1998

Trout

Headwaters

Western U.S.A.

John Gierach

"Four ponds and a dozen fair-to-middling trout later, you hook a heavy fish

back in some flooded brush – a heavy *fish. He fights well but stays in the open,*

where you play him carefully. You wish you'd brought a net, even though

you'd have snagged it in the brush two hundred times by now. You play the fish

out more than you'd like to, finally hand-landing him as gently as possible. As

you hold him by the lower jaw to remove the barbless hook, he wiggles and his

teeth cut into your thumb, starting a small stain of blood in the water."

As you follow the stream up into the canyon, it seems to get smaller and colder all at once, an illusion caused by leaving behind the civilized water where the pools are named and where there are places to park. Going upstream here, where the cliff forces the road away from the stream, feels a little like going back in time, and the trout – still mostly browns – seem as liquid and transparent as the water. You're elated, still on your first wind.

This is pocket water and there's lots of it – miles and miles of it – so rather than fish it thoroughly, you keep moving, now and then casting a dry caddis (an obscure local pattern named for the stream you're on) over a good-looking spot. It seems appropriate and it works. Later there will be a hatch of caddis or maybe even mayflies and you'll stop and get down to business, but since you're more interested in distance now, you fish casually from the bank in hiking boots with the pack on your back.

You go carefully because you're walking with the rod strung, sometimes having to thread it through the brush and low limbs ahead. The cloth bag is stuffed in your pants pocket but, in the interest of lightness and mobility, you've left the aluminum case at home.

It's your favorite cane rod, a 7½-footer for a #5 line. You debated over the choice, weighing the risk to the rod against how perfectly it was suited to this little stream. Finally the honey-colored rod with its English reel won out. It's idiotic, you thought, to spend hundreds of dollars on a fine rig you're afraid to use. And now you're pleased: the wood rod casts beautifully, and through it you can almost feel the heartbeats of the small trout. When you stop for lunch you lean it very carefully against the springy branches of a short blue spruce.

You've been walking easily and haven't gone far, but already it feels good to have the pack off. It's not as light as it could be – they never are – but considering how long you'll be out, it's not bad. You're figuring three days, maybe four, and you were very careful not to say exactly when you'd be back.

You haven't had to rummage in the pack yet, so it still seems a model of efficiency, ever so slightly virginal, leaning in the shade of a lichen-covered ledge. Tied on the top are the rolled-up sleeping pad and the poncho which can be worn to cover you and all the gear or made into a serviceable free-form rain fly. The down sleeping bag is tied to the bottom and the old number 44 "Cold Handle" frying pan is strapped securely to the back. The pan always seems a little too big, but it will hold two butterfly-filleted, eight- to twelve-inch trout perfectly. You'll eat fish on this trip or come back early; your provisions are composed of just-add-water starches and soups with some coffee, one can of pork and beans (a treat), some oil,

RIGHT *An angler selects the first fly of the morning on Nelson's Spring Creek in Montana.*

ABOVE *A Grasshopper.*

salt, pepper, and lemon juice. Side dishes. The main courses are still in the water.

Beyond that, there isn't much: clothing you can wear all at once if necessary (wool shirt, sweater, down vest, wool hat), coffeepot, fork and spoon, spare socks, flyweight waders, wading shoes (low-cut tennis shoes actually, because they're smaller and lighter than the real thing), and your tin cup. It's in the side pocket now, but if you were farther north you'd tie it next to the frying pan as a bear bell. Packed in the coffee cup is a heavy plastic bag to put the tennis shoes in once they're wet.

There's a camera in there, too, and the pack is so pretty in the mottled shade you think about digging it out and taking a shot, but it's only a thought. At the moment you don't feel like looking at the world through a piece of glass, even an expensive piece.

The only luxuries you've allowed yourself are a full-sized coffeepot, a notebook, and a modest-sized bottle of good bourbon – but maybe they're not entirely luxuries, at that. The coffeepot doubles as a saucepan, and holds enough water to completely douse the campfire in three trips to the stream. Your life has been such that there's the normal background noise of guilt, but so far, you haven't burned down a forest and don't plan to; you are meticulously careful with your fires.

The bourbon is still in the glass bottle because it just doesn't taste right from the lighter plastic flask, and whether the whiskey itself is a luxury or a necessity isn't worth worrying about at the moment. The notebook might be considered nonessential except that you generally use more of its pages to start fires than to jot down lines of poetry and notes of cosmic significance.

After lunch – a deli ham-and-cheese sandwich in waxed paper – you put the rod in the bag and walk. The trail is gone now, and the country is more rugged. Dippers splash in the stream; you spook a doe mule deer coming around a bend; and you get very close to a marmot sunning on a rock before he wakes up and bolts, giving the warning whistle, even though he seems to be alone.

At one point you find yourself within five feet of a pair of typically innocent blue grouse. You consider the possibility of getting one with a rock and have a momentary olfactory hallucination: roasting grouse and frying trout. You decide against it, though, probably because it's illegal.

And then it's late afternoon, the canyon has begun to level out a little, and the stream has a distinct shady side. The pocket water has given way to a long run, the bank on one side of which is open and grassy. There are delicious-looking undercuts. With several hours of daylight left, you find a level spot away from the stream (away from mosquitoes and morning dew or frost) and lean the pack against a tree,

unroll the sleeping bag to air out, clean out a fire pit, gather wood, and set out coffeepot, frying pan, and tin cup.

The spot you've chosen is a tiny meadow stretch only a few hundred yards long. The open sky is pleasant after the closed-in, forested canyon below, and ahead, for the first time today, you can see the snowcapped high country. The weather is still shirt-sleeve warm with a comfortable hint of evening chill. There is as much spruce and fir as pine now on the hillsides, and you can see patches of aspen. You think you hear the screech of a hawk but see nothing when you scan the sky.

You could probably fish the stream here without wading, but you dig out the waders and put them on because you carried them in and are gonna use them; it's important. There's no fly vest; instead you're wearing a four-pocketed canvas fishing shirt which you load now from the side pocket of the pack: three spools of leader material in the lower right-hand pocket, bug dope, fly floatant, and clippers in the lower left. Each breast pocket holds a fly box – one with nymphs and streamers, the other with dries. In the interest of razor-sharp efficiency, you wanted to have a single box, but the bigger ones didn't fit anywhere and you only toyed for a few minutes with the idea of rebuilding the fishing shirt. Anyhow, the bulges are more symmetrical this way.

You saw two small rises at the tail of the run when you first arrived, and now you notice what looks like a bigger fish working along the far grassy bank. There are a few tan-colored bugs that you assume are caddis flies fluttering over the surface, but without pondering the situation further, you tie on a #16 Tan-Bodied Adams. The trout in these mountain streams see few anglers and are seldom selective (though your two fly boxes are evidence of the occasional exceptions) and the Tan Adams is a favorite. The tails are of medium-dark moose body hair, the body of light raccoon fur; the grizzly hackle is mixed with ginger instead of brown and the wings are wide and darkly barred – from a hen neck. It's a personal variation you often think of as a "generic bug," an excellent high-country pattern.

You work the tail of the run first and, on the first cast, take a tiny rainbow that still has his parr marks, a wild fish. Then you take a slightly larger one that wasn't rising but came up to your fly anyway, and then you take the fish along the bank – a nine-inch brown.

The fish are eager, slightly stupid, and not large; you get a strike nearly every time you put a good cast over a rising trout. Then you land and release a fine, chubby, ten-inch brown and remember what a friend once said: "If you're gonna keep fish, go ahead and keep 'em. If you wait for the last two, you'll be eating beans." So the next good fish, a fat, bright rainbow of ten or eleven inches, is tapped

ABOVE *Sun-up on Burney Creek in California. The trout here go for tiny stoneflies and terrestrials. What to choose from the Wheatley Box?*

on the head and tossed on the bank in the direction of camp. This is something you seldom do anymore, but it doesn't feel too bad. In fact, it feels pretty good.

After five or six more fish, you take a firm brown that reaches the full twelve inches from the butt of the reel seat to the first T in the name on the rod. It's a male with a slightly hooked jaw and colors that remind you of a Midwestern autumn. You clean him, along with the rainbow, wrap them both in the wet grass, and lay them in the shadows that have now swallowed the stream and half the eastern ridge. You're camped on the west bank to catch the first morning sunlight.

You think of going to a streamer then, of running it past the undercut to see if there's a big brown there, but the dry fly and the wood rod are too hypnotic. You take a few more small fish and quit with just enough light to get situated in camp. You clip the tattered and now one-winged fly from the leader and drop it in the stream, like you'd smash a glass after a toast.

Supper is trout fried in oil with pepper and lemon juice, rice, and whiskey cut lightly with stream water – eaten by firelight. Then, lying in the down bag, you let the fire die to coals, think of the trout, the hike, home, people, career, the past, and you are asleep.

The morning is gray and cold, but blue holes perforate the clouds to the west. You put on the wool shirt and vest, build a fire, and start water for coffee. After one cup you go to the stream, waderless, and without ceremony take one nine-inch rainbow for breakfast. You roast him over the fire on a stick so as not to dirty the pan, and on another stick you make Bisquick muffins – a bit dry, but just fine. As someone (probably French) once said, "Hunger is the best sauce."

With the fire well doused and the pack loaded, you take one careful look around to make sure nothing was dropped or forgotten, then head off upstream with only a single look back at the undercut bank where you never did try a streamer.

By midmorning the sun is out, and you stop to shed some clothes before you get too sweaty. While putting the stuff in the pack, you're struck with the sudden certainty that you forgot the roll of nylon cord with which you can turn your poncho into whatever-shaped rain fly the terrain and handy trees allow; you can clearly picture it lying on the kitchen table at home. But then a short, carefully unfrantic search turns up the cord, as well as an apple you'd forgotten about. At least one attack of backpacker's paranoia per trip is normal, but you don't mind because it has served you well. You've never forgotten anything important.

With the rhythm of the walk broken, you decide to fish, and with the Tan Adams you take the first brook trout. But since you've taken only two other small fish after fifteen minutes, you shoulder the pack and move on.

ABOVE *Craig Fellin releasing a brown on the Beaverhead in Montana. An afternoon storm has just passed and beautiful Rembrandt light paints the scene. This is the time to put down the rod and grab the camera.*

RIGHT *Late summer on the Henry's Fork in Idaho brings solitude, a hint of frost in the air, and hatches of Tricos before ten o'clock. Note the Grand Tetons, Wyoming, in the background.*

Shortly you come to a road and, although it breaks the spell a little, you're glad it's there. On the way out you'll climb the grade and hitch a ride to the nearest cafe for pancakes or maybe a big, greasy burger, and then on into town. But now you go under the bridge with the stream, listening for the whine of a car and being glad not to hear one.

Above the road you come into a high, marshy meadow. Here the trees stop as the land levels out, giving way to tangles of willow; the only way to walk through it is up the stream, in waders. Wading and casting with the pack on and the hiking shoes dangling in back is clumsy but not impossible. You work only the best-looking spots at first, slowing down and concentrating a little more after you've spooked some good fish from what looked like uninteresting water. The trout are brookies now, with the occasional rainbow.

By the time you hit the beaver ponds, your back aches from the pack; so you set up camp on the first level, dry spot you come to. After a short break, you switch to

ABOVE *This old spring pond on the Hat Creek Ranch in northern California is loaded with big, fat, sassy rainbows.*

a streamer and creep down to the nearest pond. The fly is a little brook trout bucktail, and your past success with it has convinced you that brookies do, in fact, eat their smaller relatives, even though more than one fisheries biologist has told you that's not so. You think, science. *Truth.* The fish take the fly, so it's true; or maybe it's largely false but still works, and so might as well be true – like politics or religion. It occurs to you that the Great Questions are probably a hell of a lot more fun than the answers, but by the time you've made your fifth cast, you've forgotten about the whole thing.

Four ponds and a dozen fair-to-middling trout later, you hook a heavy fish in some flooded brush – a *heavy* fish. He fights well but stays in the open, where you play him carefully. You wish you'd brought a net, even though you'd have snagged it in the brush two hundred times by now. You play the fish out more than you'd like to, finally hand-landing him as gently as possible. As you hold him by the lower jaw to remove the barbless hook, he wiggles and his teeth cut into your thumb, starting a small stain of blood in the water.

Laid against the rod, the trout's tail reaches past the twelve-inch mark, well past. Sixteen inches? Possibly, and fat, too, and deeply, richly colored; the orange

BELOW *A Royal Wulff.*

BELOW *A visit to the American West wouldn't be complete without a float trip down the Yellowstone River through Paradise Valley, Montana.*

flanks are like a neon beer sign shining through a rainy night. You sit there like an idiot until the trout's struggles indicate that he's recovered from the fight. You release him then, and he swims away, leaving you with a momentary sense of absolute blankness, as if the synapses in your brain marked "good" and "bad" had fired simultaneously, shorting each other out.

Then you're hungry, and cold. You backtrack down the channel below the pond and keep the first three small trout you hook, trying to picture the exact size of the frying pan. Supper is eaten in chilly twilight; the waders are hung to dry; the rod, in its cloth case, is hung out of reach of porcupines who would chew up the cork grip

ABOVE *Freshwater springs pour down from lava outcroppings through mint, moss, and watercress to mix with snow melt from Mount Shasta at Mossbrae Falls on the Sacramento River, northern California. This is a very special place. We need to look after and protect it.*

22

for the salt, given half a chance. The dishes are washed, by feel, in muddy gravel.

The next morning you wake before dawn, soaking wet, freezing, and covered with mosquito bites, having slept dreamlessly on the edge of a bog through a substantial rain, with the poncho lying uselessly under you as a ground cloth. The curses you utter – the foulest ones you can think of – are the first words you've spoken aloud in two days.

Luckily the sky is clear now, and the sun comes up warm over the eastern ridge, helping along the effects of the smoky fire that took fifteen minutes to start. You recover by degrees, aided by coffee, and drape your gear in the willows to dry, everything angled to face the sun like the heads of flowers. Even the notebook was damp, toward the back, so you started the fire with pages that were written on, pages you did not read before lighting.

Breakfast is big and starchy, mostly half-ruined rice mixed with pond-water chicken soup, a shapeless candy bar you found while emptying the pack, and the apple. The candy-bar wrapper is burned in the fire, but the apple core is tossed in the brush for a squirrel or maybe an elk. After fluffing and turning the sleeping bag, you slog the half-mile to the head of the ponds and fish the stream, where you hook the first cutthroat – small, bright, and confused-looking. You feel a little more in touch with the place, having been soaked and frozen with, apparently, no ill effects.

Back in gear – the pack tight, dry, and efficient again – you leave the stream and hike the dry ridge toward the lake. Most of the time you can't even see the stream in its tunnels of tangled willow. You're moving well, feeling free on the dry ground in the shady spruce and fir, sensing the curves and cups of the land now instead of the bottom of the trough where the water runs.

You angle up unconsciously (almost always better to gain altitude than lose it when walking in the mountains) and come on the lake a little high, from a vantage point of no more than fifty extra feet. You wouldn't have planned that just for the view, but the view is excellent, with the small lake hanging in its tight cirque, smooth and blue-gray, with snowfields on the western slope and a soft-looking lawn of tundra around it. The trees here are short and flagged, bare of branches on the windward side.

You set up camp on a perfect, level spot, rigging a clumsy rain fly (thinking of last night) though the sky is cloudless. It seems early, *is* early, in fact, but the looming Continental Divide means dusk will come before it seems right. You stroll down to the outlet, the logical place for fish to be since the inlet is only snow melt from a scree slope, and sure enough, you spot a few rising cutts. You've tied on a #16 Michigan Chocolate Spinner, based on previous experience, time of day, location,

ABOVE *An epic struggle with a big cutthroat before a storm, on the Snake River in Wyoming.*

and hunch. You've also put on the wool shirt and hat because it's cool away from the shelter of the trees.

You stalk up to the water too quickly, too erect, and the trout don't exactly spook but solemnly stop rising. They don't know what you are, but they don't like you – a thought that cuts through the magazine-feature-article glitter of wilderness fly-fishing for the ten minutes it takes for two of the smaller fish to start feeding again.

The first cast is a good one, straight and sure with a downstream hook on the admittedly easy, uniform current, and a thirteen-inch cutt takes the spinner with a casual, unsuspicious rise. The fight is good, but because the fish has nowhere to go, you land him easily. It's supper and the last fish of the day; the others have vanished in that supernatural way trout have – they don't run like deer or fly away like grouse; they're just gone.

In camp you fry the trout, sitting close to the fire that seems to give little heat in the thin air. Camping alone isn't something you normally do, but you've done it often enough that it's familiar; you no longer get the horrors at night. You've gone out alone before because you were sad or happy, or neither or both – for any reason at all, the way some people drink. The lake is black now, and for a long moment you can't remember why you're here this time.

ABOVE *The Cassel Forebay at Clearwater House, northern California, in autumn provides good hatches and some very large fish.*

RIGHT *An angler returns home after the evening hatch on the lower Fall River in the shadow of Mount Shasta, California.*

WESTERN USA: FACTFILE

BACKGROUND

To quantify all of the western USA's trout fishing would take a lifetime of exploring. Apart from the places we feature in this book, Wyoming, Utah and Colorado are among the best states for fishing – but we have concentrated on some of the better-known streams of Montana, Idaho and northern California. These states contain classic rivers such as the Madison, Firehole, Yellowstone, Big Hole, Big Horn, Henry's Fork, Silver Creek, Hat Creek and Fall River. All have prolific hatches during the summer, and produce free-rising, selective-feeding trout, mainly rainbows and browns up to 5 or 6 lb.

All these rivers are public waterways whose sole restrictions are on the type of tackle used; many are in better condition today than they were fifty years ago; and most of the fish are wild. Although angling pressure has increased, you can find solitude easily if you look in the right places at the right times.

WHEN TO GO

Many of the best areas lie in mountainous regions, meaning that harsh winters with lots of snow are the rule. Some of the rivers are spring creeks, and their temperatures remain constant throughout the season. Generally, as the warmer summer months approach, the hatches intensify and feeding activity increases. During the cool of the morning and the late evening in midsummer, hatches often defy the imagination. There are times on the famous Henry's Fork in Idaho when it is hard to see the water for the overlapping wings of insects. During early June on Fall River, California, there appears what is known as "the carpet" – a solid mass of Pale Morning Duns, all hatching at the same time.

Often these western rivers have overlying and masking hatches, where several types of insect are hatching at the same time. The trick is to figure out exactly what the fish are feeding on. These trout can be extremely selective and difficult, and thus the best part of the season in terms of fly life can be the most demanding for a fly-fisherman.

LEFT *A.J. Derosa and Jim Sulham with a beautiful, fine-spotted Snake River cutthroat.*

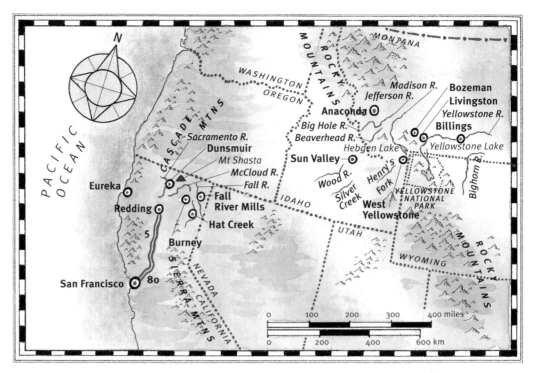

TACKLE

RODS: 9–10 ft for 4–8 wt lines, depending on the river system fished. Not all river systems will demand large rods and the wise fisherman will pack a 7 ft or 8 ft rod as well.

REELS: Direct-drive fly reels capable of holding at least 75 yards of backing.

LINES: A weight-forward floater will be very useful. However, a sink-tip and full sinking lines of different densities will have their moments, particularly early in the season.

LEADERS: Long and fine leaders are needed to approach selective feeders with the dry fly: 9–18 ft tapered to as light as 1.5 lb test. Shorter leaders for fishing wet flies: 8–12 ft tapered to 3 lb maximum.

FLIES: Dry flies – Parachute Adams, Tricos, Royal Wulff, Yellow Humpy, Pale Morning Dun and Goddard Caddis. Nymphs – Wooly Bugger, Zugbug, Muskrat and Pheasant Tail. Streamers – Renegade, Zonker, White and Black Marabou.

FLIES 1 *Royal Wulff* 2 *Stimulator* 3 *Humpy Adams* 4 *Gray Wulff* 5 *Perla Stone* 6 *Green Drake Wulff* 7 *Black Wulff* 8 *Yellow Humpy* 9 *Black Stone* 10 *Living Damsel*

His Biggest Trout

England

J.W. Hills

"I was about to reel up when a fish rose ten yards above, close under my bank. It was one of those small movements difficult to place. It might be a very large fish or a very small one. A wild thought swept through me that this was my big one: but no, I said to myself, it cannot be. This is not where he was rising. Besides, things do not happen like that, except in books: it is only in books that you make a fearful bungle and go back later and see a small break which you think is a dace, and cast carelessly and hook something the size of an autumn salmon ..."

Those who fish rivers where mayfly come will agree that, though with it you get a higher average weight, yet actually the biggest fish are killed on the sedge. In 1903 on the Kennet [it] was a great mayfly season for heavy fish, and a friend of mine who had the Ramsbury water got the truly remarkable bag of six fish in one day which weighed over nineteen pounds: and yet the two heaviest fish of the year were got on the sedge. I got the heaviest. It was the 26 July 1903, a cloudy, gusty day, with a downstream wind, and I was on the water from eleven to five without seeing a rise. My friend and I then had tea and walked up the river at a quarter past six. Olives began to appear and trout to move; and suddenly a really large one started rising. We stood and watched, with growing excitement. He was taking every fly, in solid and determined fashion, and the oftener he appeared the bigger he looked, and the faster beat our hearts. It was settled that I was to try for him. I was nervous and uncomfortable. He was very big: it was a long throw and the wind horrible: I could not reach him, and like a fool I got rattled and pulled off too much line: there was an agonized groan from my friend behind me when a great curl of it was slapped on the water exactly over the trout's nose. We looked at each other without speaking, and he silently walked away up the river, leaving me staring stupidly at the spot where the trout had been rising. Of course he was gone.

The next two hours can be passed over. The small fly rise came and went. I caught a trout on a No. 2 silver sedge and finally, at about a quarter past eight, found myself gazing gloomily at the place where I had bungled. The wild wind had

BELOW *A Green Drake.*

OPPOSITE BELOW *An old stone bridge over the River Avon in Wiltshire has harbored many large trout in its shadows.*

BELOW *A quiet woodland pool on the upper Bourne in Hampshire offers a chance for a reflective moment to a passing angler.*

blown itself out and had swept the sky bare of cloud. Silence had come, and stillness. The willows, which all through the long summer day had bowed and
chattered in the wind, were straightened and motionless, each individual leaf hanging down as though carved in jade: the forest of great sedges, which the gusts had
swept into wave after wave of a roaring sea of emerald, was now calm and level,
each stalk standing straight and stiff as on a Japanese screen. There had occurred
that transition, that transmutation from noise and movement to silence and peace,
which would be more wonderful were we not so accustomed to it, when a windy
summer day turns over to a moveless summer night: when the swing and clatter
and rush of the day is arrested and lifted from the world, and you get the sense that
the great hollow of the air is filled with stillness and quiet, as with a tangible presence. They are peaceful things, these summer evenings after wild days, and I
remember particularly that this was one of the most peaceful; more so indeed than
my thoughts, which were still in a turmoil. I stood watching mechanically, and
then, tempting fate to help me, made a cast or two over the spot where the fish had
been. How easy it was to reach it now, how lightly my fly settled on the water, how
gracefully it swung over the place. All to no purpose, of course, for nothing
happened, and I was about to reel up when a fish rose ten yards above, close under
my bank. It was one of those small movements difficult to place. It might be a very
large fish or a very small one. A wild thought swept through me that this was my big
one: but no, I said to myself, it cannot be. This is not where he was rising. Besides,
things do not happen like that, except in books: it is only in books that you make a
fearful bungle and go back later and see a small break which you think is a dace, and

ABOVE *Nick Zoll fishing above Broadlands House on the River Test in Hampshire during a mayfly hatch.*

cast carelessly and hook something the size of an autumn salmon: it is only in books that fate works in such fashion. Why, I know it all so well that I could write it out by heart, every move of it. But this is myself by a river, not reading in a chair. This is the real world, where such things do not happen: that is the rise of a half-pound trout.

I cast. I was looking right into the west, and the water was coloured like skim milk by reflection from where the sun had set. My silver sedge was as visible as by day. It floated down, there was a rise, I struck, and something rushed upstream. Then I knew.

Above me was open water for some twenty-five yards, and above that again a solid block of weed, stretching right across. My fish made for this, by short, irresistible runs. To let him get into it would have been folly: he must be stopped: either he is well hooked or lightly, the gut is either sound or rotten: kill or cure, he must be turned, if turned he can be: so I pulled hard, and fortunately got his head round and led him down. He played deep and heavy and I had to handle him roughly, but I brought him down with a smash, and I began to breathe again. But then another terror appeared. In the place we had reached the only clear water

ABOVE *This tiny braid of the River Bourne harbors some especially nice wild browns.*

ABOVE *Spotting a quietly rising trout on the River Itchen, Hampshire, in the shade of a willow requires patience and a keen eye.*

was a channel under my bank, and the rest of the river was choked with weed. Should I try to pull him down this channel, about three or four yards wide, to the open water below? No. It was much too dangerous, for the fish was uncontrollable, and if he really wanted to get to weed he would either get there or break me: even with a beaten fish it would be extremely risky, and with an unbeaten one it was unthinkable. Well, if he would not come down he must go up, and up he went willingly enough, for when I released pressure he made a long rush up to the higher weed bed, whilst I ran up the meadow after him, and with even greater difficulty turned him once more. This time I thought he was really going right through it, so fast and so heavy was his pull, and I think he was making for a hatch hole above: but once more my gallant gut stood the strain and, resisting vigorously, he was led down again. This proceeding was repeated either two or three times more, I forget which: either three or four times we fought up and down that twenty-five yards of river. By then he was tiring, and I took up my station in the middle of the stretch, where I hoped to bring him in: my hand was actually on the sling of the net when he suddenly awoke and rushed up. He reached the weed bed at a pace at which it was impossible to stop, shot into it like a torpedo, and I had the sickening certainty that I should lose him after all. To hold him hard now would be to make a smash certain, so I slacked off: when he stopped I tightened again, expecting miserably to feel the dead, lifeless drag of a weeded line. Instead, to my delight, I found I was still in contact with the fish, and he was pulling hard. How he had carried the line through the weeds I do not know. To look at it seemed impossible.... But the line was clear, and the fish proved it by careering wildly on towards the hatch, making the reel sing. I believe he meant to go through into the carrier, as fish have done

BELOW *Thomas Yellow May.*

before and after, but I turned him. However, we could not stay where we were. The hatch was open at the bottom, there was a strong draw through it, and if a heavy, beaten fish got into this, no gut would hold him up. At all risks he must be taken over the weed into the clear water. I pulled him up to the top and ran him down. Then, for the first time after so many perils, came the conviction that I should land him. He was obviously big, but how big could not be known, for I had not had a clear sight of him yet. He still pulled with that immovable, quivering solidity only shown by a very heavy fish. But at last even his great strength tired. He gave a wobble or two, yielded, and suddenly he was splashing on the top, looking huge in the dusk. There ensued that agonizing time when you have a big fish nearly beat,

but he is still too heavy to pull in, and nothing you can do gets him to the net. At last I pulled him over to it, but I lifted too soon, the ring caught in the middle of the body, he wavered a moment in the air and then toppled back into the water with a sickening splash. A judgment, I thought, and for a shattering second I believed he had broken the gut, but he was still on. I was pretty well rattled by then and, in the half light, made two more bad shots, but the end came at last, he was in the net and on the bank.

How big was he? Three pounds? Yes, and more. Four pounds? Yes, and more. Five? He might be, he might. My knees shook and my fingers trembled as I got him on the hook of the steelyard. He weighed a fraction over four pounds eight ounces.

ENGLAND: FACTFILE

BACKGROUND

The English chalkstreams are for many the true birthplace of modern methods of fishing with dry fly and nymph, now adopted by fishermen in rivers around the world. The chalkstreams still hold a certain magic in the minds of all fishermen, and fishing here you know that you are walking in the footsteps of some of fly-fishing's legends. Wild brown trout fishing can still be found here at its best and most demanding.

Though wild fish densities are not as high as they were in Izaak Walton's day and genetic purity is in some places challenged, it should not be forgotten that these fish are the forebears of many of the world's brown trout populations. The reputation that wild chalkstream brown trout have of testing the skill of a modern angler is well earned and has not diminished in the slightest. The beauty of the surroundings serves to create a fishing idyll that has existed for generations, and sitting on the bank of a chalkstream in June remains one of the highlights of fly-fishing.

WHEN TO GO

The season starts in mid-April, but generally the best of the fishing begins in May with the onset of summer and of the serious fly hatches. The classic mayfly hatch, on beats where it exists, generally occurs toward the end of May and the beginning of June. While this is the most popular and heavily fished hatch of the year, the trout develop a more discerning palate throughout the rest of the season.

Upstream fishing is the only legal method of fishing on most beats. Nymphs are generally forbidden until the middle of July, and on some beats their use is prohibited completely. The best of the season is over by the end of September, but fine autumn weather can prolong daytime hatches by another week or two.

TOP LEFT *A fishing party waits for the mayfly hatch to begin above Broadlands House on the River Test.*

BOTTOM LEFT *A beautiful wild Itchen brown about to be released.*

FLIES 1 *Claret Sedge*
2 *Spent Gnat*
3 *Thomas Yellow May*
4 *Houghton Ruby*
5 *Pink Shrimp*
6 *Richard Walker Sedge* 7 *Green Drake*
8 & 9 *Tup's Indispensables*
10 *Greenwell's Glory*

TACKLE

RODS: Depending on the size of the stream, 7–9 ft single-handed rods for a 2–4 wt line.

REELS: Basic direct-drive fly reel to balance with chosen rod.

LINES: Floating lines, 2–4 wt.

LEADERS: The lighter the better, and rarely more than 4X (4 lb) breaking strain is necessary.

FLIES: Match the hatch, which can change quickly. Proven favourites include: March Browns, Grannom and Hawthorns early in the year; Mayfly, Greenwell's Glory, Black Gnat, Tup's Indispensable, Olives, Sedge (caddis) patterns later in the year. Nymphs might include Hare's Ear, Pheasant Tail, Grey Goose and Shrimp.

There can be tremendous variation in hatches of fly from one beat to another, as well as from river to river, and it is generally wise to enquire which hatches are predominating on your stretch prior to fishing it.

Mighty Mask

Ireland

David Street

"The wind was fine for dapping and patches of sunlight were starting to penetrate the clouds; if there was ever a time to fish the bluebottle, this was it. Bill changed rods and was soon dapping with the first of our two bluebottles. On the top of a rolling wave and against the vast expanses of the lough, it looked absurdly small, but, even at the distance he was fishing it, we could see the radiant splendours of its colours. Then, within minutes, a small circle showed on the wave's crest where the bluebottle had been riding – so quietly did the trout take."

ABOVE *A portrait of Dennis O'Keefe, my boatman and companion on Lough Sheelin, and his fly box. Both are truly exceptional – even brilliant – and I will never forget either one.*

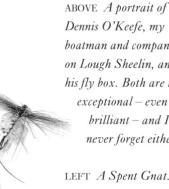

LEFT *A Spent Gnat.*

Of the big limestone loughs on the western chain my favourite has to be Lough Mask to the north of Corrib – surely one of the world's great trout waters. On its eastern flank stretch the green plains of Mayo, which roll as pleasingly as the soft brogue on the local tongue. Above its western shore the blue Partry Mountains stand guard with the peaks of Joyce's Country showing clearly to the south. It is a vast expanse of water covering some 20,500 acres in all, ten miles long with an average width of around four miles.

It carries many enchanting islands as well as great reefs of rock which, being limestone, are jagged and needle-sharp, and some of these reach far into the middle waters of the lough, where one might expect the deepest places to be. Here they lie hidden just beneath the surface and sharp enough to pierce clean through the boat, making Mask no place for a newcomer to go charging about with an outboard engine.

There are days when the barometer rides high and the water looks innocuous enough, as it shimmers in a mirror-calm, but the weather can change quickly, as high winds sweep down from the Partry Mountains to transform it into a surging sea. The true Mask fisherman not only knows his lough in great detail, but also holds it always in a deep respect. It is, however, the presence of these reefs and shallows that makes the fishing, for they provide those superb long drifts over waters, varying in depth from three to ten feet, where trout to four pounds and more come readily to the fly.

It was Bill's invitation to join him at Ballinrobe for a week's fishing at the end of June that was my first introduction to the joys of Mask. Ballinrobe is a typical Irish country market town of much character and, by virtue of its position, in the middle of the eastern shore with its extensive shallows and rocky outcrops, is the natural centre for the fishing.

I joined him in Dublin and together we drove across Ireland, arriving in time to secure a boat for the week – Bill had his own outboard – and pick up a cylinder of Calor gas before pitching our tent in the soft evening rain by Caher Bay. Our routine was pretty basic and designed to give us maximum fishing time. The morning shave, bacon and egg breakfast, followed by a quick run into town to keep the camp larder stocked. I say "stocked" because our adversary turned out to be a stray dog, who prowled around our tent like the hosts of Midian, his mission to turn over our bin and to unstock our larder as quickly as he could. He had a great appetite for our steak suppers. With the chores completed, sandwiches made, camp secured and dog seen off, we would spend the day fishing our teams of wet flies down the long drifts of the lough.

Lunch would be taken on one of the many islands where we brewed the tea and sat amongst the random scatterings of limestone chips, which lay all around us, sharp and deeply fissured, and in all kinds of grotesque shapes. Cleaned and nicely mounted, some could have passed as works of modern sculpture. Bill, who has never lacked an eye for a quick bargain, set one up in the sand behind the fire and proclaimed it "The Violin Player", an early piece by Henry Moore, and I could see exactly what he meant. Sometimes other boats would be taking lunch as well, and it was good to compare notes on the morning's sport, and listen to improbable stories. Tea was always brewed in the "Volcano", an aptly named contraption that I have only ever found in Ireland. It is made of tin, the top part being filled with water from the lough and the base containing the little stick fire. Even on wet days the water comes quickly to the boil with the help of a little petrol from the outboard; the fresh tea has a tang about it that is far superior to the stuff from a thermos flask. I am sure the old Irish tinkers used to make them, and I would dearly love to get my hands on one. In my mind they are an integral part of a day's boat-fishing on the lough.

From his earlier exploits Bill had come to know the local boatmen – he was one of their number – as well as most of the fishing fraternity in the town, many of whom would gather for the evening jar in Luke's bar; and it was there that our footsteps would lead us before the day was out.

By the time we arrived at Luke's pub, it was as busy and full as ever. Luke was a fine-looking man of a somewhat military appearance and both he and his wife, Eileen, were excellent hosts. The bar they kept was full of character too, always dimly lit with ancient firearms glinting from the walls, for Luke was a keen collector of curios. It was a place of warmth and friendliness where conversation was what mattered – no nonsense here of fruit-machines or piped music. Luke was also a keen fisherman – he could hardly have been otherwise – with a special fond-ness for Lough Carra, a much smaller lough half a mile to the north-east of Mask.

I have heard Carra described as the most alkaline lake in Europe and I can well believe it. Its water is exceedingly clear, which is often disconcerting when you are fishing, as you tend to see the fish before they take the fly. The lough floor is a white sand and the rocks in the water are covered by a thick deposit of a soft, spongy marl, as if nature had fitted them with fenders. If you happen to hit a rock on Lough Mask it will possibly pierce the boat, but on Carra it is the rock that will be dented. The overall colour of the water is a yellowy green, like weak lime-juice, with the shades varying according to the depth, and much of the shoreline is fringed with large beds of reed.

ABOVE *An antique mayfly box, used originally for collecting live insects for dapping.*

There were other evenings when Bill and I went straight to the pub after supper, before setting out once more on Mask to fish the sedge. After the day-time fishing it was somewhat eerie to be creeping under silent oars into Ballinachalla Bay by the light of the stars, and almost frightening to hear the massive trout erupting as they came for these sedges – some of them would have been fish in the five- or six-pound class. We both tied on Green Peters and fished them dry, even though it was no longer possible to see them on the water. Sometimes we drew the fly across the top, in imitation of the living creature, as it jerked its way in stages across the surface. When it is too dark to see the fly, I suppose one ought to strike each time a fish rises in the area where one thinks one's fly to be, and failing to do this, I probably missed the one chance I had, but, exciting as it was, we were not successful and returned fishless to our tent.

Irish fishermen on these big loughs are a thoroughly conservative breed, who rely almost wholly on fishing down the drifts with a team of three wet flies, or else dapping with the live insect, whilst a smaller number seem content with the tedious employment of trolling. They are reluctant to experiment, try a variation of tactics or do anything that diverges from this norm, even on those occasions when the well-tried methods fail to bring results. The dry fly, for instance, is virtually ignored. There is, however, some justification for this, because, as a general rule, the dry fly is always likely to be more effective on the smaller loughs. On the huge expanses, such as Mask affords, what hatches of fly there may be will be very localized affairs, and, provided there is a wave on the water, fish which may be rising will come to the wet flies just as well.

There remain, however, certain types of conditions – calm, bright days – when small dry flies do provide for better (and sometimes the only) opportunities for fish. Bill and I discovered this on just such a day one late August when the surface of the lough reflected like a mirror. As we motored up to Lively Bay we could spot occasional rises here and there, but they were few and far between and suggested cruising fish. We had decided to try the very small flies off a rocky shoreline, where we had some help from the sporadic appearances of the faintest of breezes which, when it was there, was just enough to put a little pin-ripple on the water. Within the

ABOVE *I couldn't resist composing this shot in celebration of a great day's fishing out on the lough during the mayfly hatch.*

hour, we each had a trout of over two pounds – Bill's to a size 16 Ant and mine to an equally small Ginger Quill. On days like these, most boats remain tied up and the few that are out will be trolling, but we met up with one, which contained two of Mask's specialists, who had been persevering with traditional wet flies, if not with much hope, and they were amazed that such tiny flies had worked.

Lough Mask has now become firmly established as the venue for the annual World Cup Wet-Fly Trout Angling Championship, and 1985 witnessed the twenty-first running of this event on these waters. From fairly modest beginnings of eighty to ninety rods in the early years, the reputation and popularity of these championships have grown steadily, and a new record of 371 anglers, from many countries, competed in 1985.

A fly-fishing competition that supports such a grandiose title has to be something special, and this one certainly qualifies. A combination of two factors – one of the world's great wild trout waters, and skilled boatmen – makes for a promising enough beginning, and many of the boatmen are truly colourful characters, to fish in whose company is an experience in itself. Not only do they know the lough like they know the way upstairs, but the fact that they are themselves competing each day for the Best Boatman prize ensures that they will work hard for their fishermen. Boatmen and anglers are all there to win. Such competition fishing is not for me. I have nothing against it in principle; it is only that the art I learnt as a boy I now pursue for relaxation. It is my way of easing the tensions that build up, restoring the harmonies and finding wholeness where waters softly lap.

When the Almighty had done creating Corrib and Mask and all the other fine big loughs of Ireland, He then had to make people to fish on them. To achieve this He must first have·shaped three moulds, one for the trolling man, one for the dapping man and one for the fisher of flies. The trolling man turned out broad in the shoulder with a distinctly hunched appearance, the dapping man carried more flesh and made excellent ballast in the boat, and the fly-caster was more lithe than either and much quicker in reaction. Of course, in the long chain of evolution, many of us have become true hybrids, multifarious fishermen.

The hero of my story is none other than the humble bluebottle or blowfly – call him what you will – and, though he sports no claim to be a classic dapping bait, he can nonetheless prove himself a very deadly man for trout, and he certainly has his day. Bill had known this all his life, for, as a lad in the English North Country, he had learnt his fishing on the many little rills and becks that run among the hills there.

He grew to know their secret places – deep holes beneath the bushes, where the dark waters had, in times of flood, eaten their way in under banks. These provided the most desirable residences in the streams and were occupied by the best trout, who grew fatter each summer as the breezes blew many insects on to the water from the boughs above. In such sanctuaries, though a worm or minnow trundled down the run might reach them, they were generally safe enough from the angler's fly.

With cat-like tread Bill had stalked these trout until he could just manage to poke his rod-tip through the branches and lower a natural bluebottle on to the water. Being only feet away from the quarry, this kind of fishing demanded great skill, perfect judgment and the patience of Job, as entanglements were frequent, to say nothing of the difficulties involved in landing a fish, once hooked. It was, never-theless, an excellent school, for those who can winkle out trout by such methods can surely catch them anywhere.

The bluebottle, of course, has earned himself a thoroughly bad name, and most people regard him as no more than a pest and a threat to the hygiene of the kitchen. He rouses up that killer instinct which is never far below the surface in any of us, though I sometimes wonder if those perfumed sprays, which the housewife now uses, are not more harmful still. Whether we like him or not, he remains a creature of great beauty, whose iridescent, green-blue body reflects like a jewel with the glint of sunlight upon it. Boyhood forays apart, we had neither of us thought seriously about the bluebottle from a fishing point of view until it happened more or less by accident.

Nearing the end of our week's fishing holiday, we decided one warm evening that we would go into Ballinrobe for our dinner, to give ourselves a break from the chores of cooking in the tent. Except for one other guest, we had the dining room at the Railway Hotel to ourselves and, with the meal finished, were taking our time over coffee and enjoying a cigar. The hotel waitress, presumably also enjoying a quiet evening, had not yet removed our dirty dinner plates, which soon attracted a large bluebottle, whose appearance must have kindled former triumphs in Bill's mind. After paying our bill, we left the hotel, taking with us two bluebottles in a matchbox.

We had completely forgotten about the wretched creatures when we set out on the lough next morning, where the trout proved hard to move; two undersized fish were all we took in the first two hours. We had just started a new drift down a shore not very far from the entrance to Caher Bay, when Bill looked for a match to light his cigar, and suddenly remembered that the box in his pocket had other tenants.

The wind was fine for dapping and patches of sunlight were starting to pene-trate the clouds; if there was ever a time to fish the bluebottle, this was it. Bill

ABOVE *Lunchtime on the Irish loughs is as much a part of the experience of trout fishing in Ireland as the fishing itself. It's a time for fishermen to gather and talk tactics and tall stories.*

changed rods and was soon dapping with the first of our two bluebottles. On the top of a rolling wave and against the vast expanses of the lough, it looked absurdly small, but, even at the distance he was fishing it, we could see the radiant splendours of its colours. Then, within minutes, a small circle showed on the wave's crest where the bluebottle had been riding – so quietly did the trout take. Bill did all the right things, lowering his rod-point, allowing plenty of time, and was soon playing a handsome fish, which was safely boated.

Now he passed the rod to me, remarking curtly as he did so, "Your turn, and remember we've only one left, so don't go messing things up."

This second and last bluebottle produced what was virtually a repeat performance, bringing me a fine two-and-a-half-pound trout, which appeared to be an identical twin to the one we already had in the boat. A pair of blowflies from the dirty dinner plates, a glimpse of sunshine, twenty minutes' fishing time and five pounds of trout – that was not bad going.

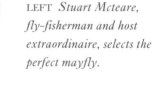

We then landed for lunch and the search began for more bluebottles, but we never even saw one, and, in any case, I would defy most people to catch one in the open air. Our arrival, however, had attracted the local cows, which soon gathered round to inspect us. The nearest thing we could get to a bluebottle was the cowdung fly and these were there in plenty, but our efforts to catch them were also in vain. Their name betrays their habitat, and all we succeeded in doing was to add a strange new flavour to our sandwiches. Even if we had got one he would not have been the same man at all.

The following day we went back into Ballinrobe just in order to stock up with bluebottles, but had quite forgotten it was early closing, and all the shops were shut when we arrived. We stood and stared longingly outside the butcher's window, where the thickness of a pane of glass was all that separated us from the finest bluebottles one could have wished for. I suppose that was hardly surprising since they must have been feeding on some of the best steaks in Mayo. A maggot-farmer would have had to go a long way to find breeding stock of this kind of quality.

Perhaps it was just as well the shop was closed, for it is one thing to enter a butcher's and ask for meat, but probably quite another to ask for the blow-flies only. One man's shame can be another's gold, and, as we headed out into the lough, we carried no such gold. It was, of course, our final day, and one which the sun kept breaking through to gild, as if to tantalize still further the fishers of the humble bluebottle.

BELOW *Lough Sheelin in the magical last hour of light – when big trout start to prowl and a fisherman's pulse begins to race.*

IRELAND: FACTFILE

BACKGROUND

Piscator non solum piscatur: "There is more to fishing than catching fish." Or so goes the motto from the famous Flyfishers Club in London. None of the other destinations featured in this book encapsulates these sentiments so precisely as does Ireland, where the wit and wisdom of your boatman and the daily ritual of lunch and tea on an isolated island are as integral a part of the fishing as tying on your fly.

While Ireland has its fair share of salmon and trout rivers, it is perhaps for the trout loughs (lakes) in the midlands and on the west coast that it is best known. These great lakes lie in the limestone bedrock of Ireland and with their high pH factor create a proliferation of insect life which in turn nourishes the trout at an extraordinary rate. Sheelin is reckoned to have the highest natural growth rate for brown trout in a still-water, anywhere in Europe.

The average size of fish on most loughs is about 2 lb, but on some, such as Sheelin, it can be as high as 4 lb. These leopard-spotted, golden-bellied trout, though, do not become large by being stupid, and they can be extremely difficult to catch. Perhaps the best line of attack when they are proving dour is to retreat to one of the many lakeside pubs and think things through over a pint of Guinness. One thing is for sure: some of Europe's largest wild trout will be waiting for you and your boatman when you return to the lough.

WHEN TO GO

Main fly hatches on most of the loughs start off each year with midge hatches in March. Shortly afterwards, in April, come the duckfly and lake olive hatches. The fishing pace on all Irish trout loughs reaches its most frenetic around the second week of May, with the advent of the mayfly, which for many is the highlight of the season. The mayfly is mostly over by early June and the fish become difficult to tempt to the surface as they start to hunt the schools of fry that abound in most loughs. Not

LEFT *Myself with a beautiful 5 lb Lough Sheelin brown, caught at twilight on a Murrough with the first cast.*

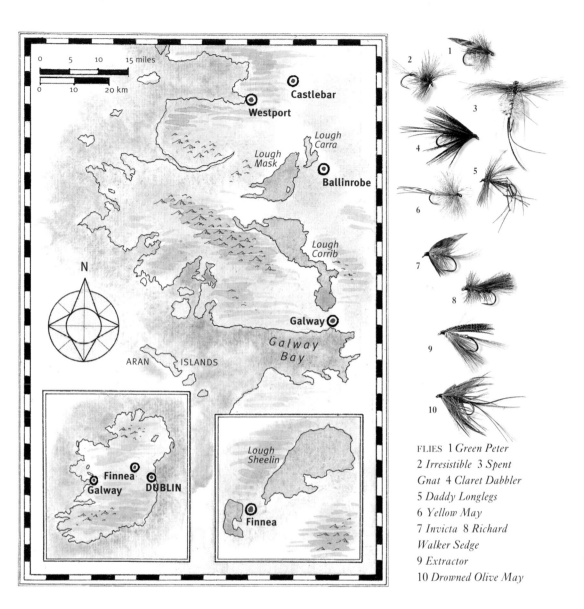

FLIES 1 *Green Peter*
2 *Irresistible* 3 *Spent Gnat* 4 *Claret Dabbler*
5 *Daddy Longlegs*
6 *Yellow May*
7 *Invicta* 8 *Richard Walker Sedge*
9 *Extractor*
10 *Drowned Olive May*

until late July, August and September can they once again be teased up to partake of the bloodworm, large sedges (caddis), daddy longlegs (craneflies) and grasshoppers. It is relatively easy to arrange for a boat on all the loughs, but it is wise to book accommodation in advance, particularly in May.

TACKLE

RODS: Single-handed 9–11 ft for 5–7 wt lines.

REELS: Direct-drive reels to balance with rod.

LINES: Almost exclusively floating line but take intermediate and sinking-tips.

LEADERS: Not less than 6 lb and up to 10 lb.

FLIES: Seasonal variations will, naturally, apply, but proven favourites include: Duckfly, Mayfly (Wulff or Shadow), Green Peter and Murrough Sedges, Bumble patterns (Claret, Golden and Olive), Fiery Brown, Kingsmill, Invicta, Teal Blue and Silver, Bloodworm, Hoppers and Daddy Longlegs.

Casting off the Edge of the World

Argentina

"There were many memorable fish. There was the great fish that leapt clean on to the distant bank to take its bearings when it was hooked, and that then leapt immediately back into the water ready for the fight. There was the fish that leapt above my head while I was wading chest-deep and that trailed rubies behind it through the red, setting sun."

It must have been as a boy that the name first stuck. I do not know what the map was; or who the author was, if it was a book, but it seems as though the name has always been there, lodged in my imagination like a flaming arrow. Tierra del Fuego! Land of Fire! What images the name conjures up. Volcanoes, maybe, and red, spilling lava; or natives on a headland, silhouetted against flames. In my mind, in many minds, the name is synonymous with the remotest place the imagination can grasp. Tierra del Fuego, the very end of the world.

Nothing much can change in that extraordinary place, nothing much about it can alter. Jets, though, are bringing it nearer. Now flights carrying anglers arrive there most weeks in the Southern autumn before the hounds of Cape Horn slip their leash. The planes come down from Buenos Aires, partly over coast, partly over hazed deserts. They touch down at Rio Grande airport at the mouth of the Rio Grande river, the most famous sea-trout river in the world.

I once fished the Rio Grande for a week. It was a week that came flooding back to me, in tiny detail, long afterwards, thanks to a mishap in the post....

My young grandson was thrilled with his new car transporter. He was playing with it when he asked if Father Christmas had come to my house too. As it happens, Father Christmas did come. He popped a small package through my letter box. It contained what a film-processing laboratory had long since claimed it had never received: a set of transparencies shot in Tierra del Fuego.

The pictures cleared away the haze of distance and time. One brought back every detail of one of the most memorable hour's fishing that I have ever had. Another provided proof-positive of a sea trout beyond imagining.

It is a long time since I fished the Rio Grande. The river lies like a crack across the coccyx of South America's spine. It flows through desolately beautiful, limitlessly horizoned plains, more or less due east from the Andes. It empties into the South Atlantic, more or less midway between the Magellan Straits and Cape Horn.

I fished from Kau Tapen Lodge, twenty miles inland on a rolling dirt road. There were six of us there: three Argentinians, two Americans and me. We fished singly or in pairs, always with a professional guide armed with spare flies and a vast landing net that had a powerful spring balance built into the handle.

The fishing, in spite of the renowned size of the Rio Grande's sea trout, was all with single-handed trout rods. I used a seven-weight, nine-foot carbon rod equipped with a butt extension to take some strain off my wrist, a large-capacity disc-braked reel and, most of the time, a weight-forward, fast sinking line.

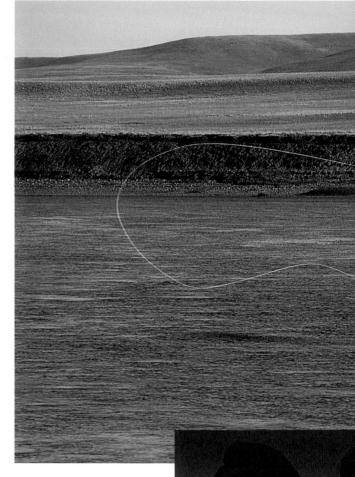

ABOVE *Tom McGuane casting for sea trout on the Villa Maria Water of the Rio Grande.*

RIGHT *A late-evening fly change on the Rio Grande. It is in these final moments before pitch black that the sea trout seem to throw caution to the wind as they aggressively attack the fly.*

RIGHT *An* asado, *or barbecue, with lamb and red wine after the evening fishing.*

The line had as much to do with the wind as the water. The Rio Grande is easily wadable on most reaches and most of the water is briskly paced, perfect for the fly. In calm weather, a floating line would have been a delight to use; but, when I was there, the wind blew almost without relent. It became a living, bullying thing. It whistled about my rod as through a ship's rigging, it flapped my waterproofs about my head like loose sails. The wind whipped tears from my eyes, impressed itself on my cheeks, moved the very ears on my head when it gusted from behind.

When the wind was up, the narrow, heavy sinking line was needed as much to help me cast as to sink close to the bottom. It was, though, part of the experience: the challenge was to work with the wind and not to struggle against it.

When the wind dropped, which it did from time to time, we shared the high, wide skies with spiralling condors and noisesome flights of Magellan geese. We shared the honey-coloured plains with honey-coloured guanacos, llama-like animals that studied us hair-triggered, edgily curious. We shared the water with the muskrats and the beavers and the fish.

My fear had been that I would arrive too soon; that coming in early January in a season that runs from January to the end of March would see me miss the main runs. Yet the river was already full of fish, now rolling and sploshing, now winking silver, now sullenly lying doggo in the long, wide pools.

There are rivers quite like the River Grande in Alaska: wide sweeps of rivers that are filled with salmon from bed to surface and bank to bank when the height of the season comes; but, in Alaska at these times, the fishing is easy. It can be a fish each cast and it is not so much the energy that needs to be paced, but the day.

Here, although there were fish in great numbers, they were more dispersed and had to be worked for. We each caught our share, but they were mostly hard-won.

And what fish! In most rivers in Great Britain that contain sea trout, the fish average around one pound, approaching maybe two. A three-pounder is a nice one, friends hear of four-pounders, five-pounders are noted on Christmas cards to old angling enemies.

In six full days and one evening on the Rio Grande, I caught twenty-three sea trout – by no means an exceptional score. The smallest weighed five pounds. The average was just a fraction under ten pounds. The largest was – well, very large.

The fish came at first in ones and twos, the daily score gradually creeping up as the week progressed, which is the proper way for any fishing week to unfold.

There were many memorable fish. There was the great fish that leapt clean on to the distant bank to take its bearings when it was hooked, and that then leapt immediately back into the water ready for the fight. There was the fish that

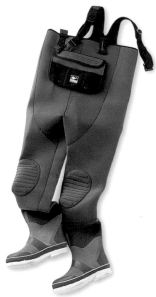

ABOVE *During a windy late afternoon a determined angler sets forth for the Rio Gallegos, a "hot" new sea-trout destination.*

leapt above my head while I was wading chest-deep and that trailed rubies behind it through the red, setting sun.

Above all there were the fish in the photographs: the one recalling a moment in the best day I had, the other freezing for ever that sea trout of my lifetime.

The best day began on a long pool with a high bank opposite. It was, my guide said, usually fished from the near bank at the upstream end. I said that for all the awkwardness of the high bank for casting, I favoured the side opposite, at the pool's lower end. To some head-shaking and what I like to think was mere tut-tutting in Spanish, I waded over. With the first cast, I hit a fish that shattered the surface at once and came off. Second cast, I had a solid pull but failed to connect. Third cast, I had a take so violent that it pulled my heart into my mouth.

I stumbled and splashed downstream behind an unseen force, tripped over a branch that lay white and bleached as an old bone and eventually landed the trout. We slipped out the barbless hook, my American companion took the photograph of the sea trout, my guide and me that I am looking at now – and then we returned the prize to the water, as we did with every catch that week. It had weighed thirteen pounds.

I made my way back to the same casting spot. Another cast, another thumping take, another rod-creaking, breathless fight. A ten-pounder. Next cast, a missed fish. The cast after that, a fish that took with such immense, sudden power that I found myself looking at a shattered line streaming head-high, downwind.

A new leader, a new fly, a new cast and a new fish, a cart-wheeling seven-pounder that was thirty yards downstream before I could gather up the loose line and follow. All of this, all of it, in less than an hour and still another thirteen-pounder and another five-pounder to come.

The great fish came on my last day. It came from the neck of a deep, fast pool: a broad-shouldered, barrel-chested monster of a fish that was impossibly thick right down to the tail. It took for ever to land, time after time turning away from the net and bow-waving across the shallows towards the middle; but eventually he tired. I laid the fish gently on the grass, put my rod beside it to give some measure of scale, and took out my camera. Click. Seventeen pounds precisely.

That fish was as exhausted as I was. I can see myself now nursing it back to strength, holding it upright facing the current. I begin to feel it flex and shrug, see its pectoral fins gradually extend and splay; watch as it gulps oxygen steady and slow; and then the great tail sweeps aside my holding hands and the fish is gone, heading for its destiny in the foothills of the Andes.

So yes, I told my grandson, Father Christmas did come to my house this year. He came in a blue uniform, in broad daylight, on a bicycle; and he brought me a transporter, too.

BELOW *In the gathering gloom of twilight Yvon Chouinard punches out another cast aimed at the far bank, where sea trout can be heard if not seen.*

ARGENTINA: FACTFILE

BACKGROUND

With its high altitude, cold-flowing, clean rivers, little or no natural predation or pollution, and very low human density, Argentine Patagonia had always been a vast network of catchments waiting to become trout fisheries. Abundant varieties of oxygenating weed for cover, and large densities of freshwater crustaceans and insect life for food, ensured the perfect environment in which to nurture trout. Between the late 1920s and the early 1930s fertilized trout and salmon ova were shipped to Argentina from North America and Europe.

Original stocks of fish included Atlantic salmon, and rainbow, brook and brown trout. In the southern half of Patagonia the most successful strains of fish were the Loch Leven and Thames strain brown trout, brought from England. In addition to a non-migratory river-trout population, a sea-going race of these fish established themselves in the Rio Grande, Rio Gallegos and several smaller rivers by the mid-1950s. Joe Brooks, the legendary American angler, first publicized these fish in the late 1950s and early 1960s, and visiting anglers began to fish for them.

With the advent of catch-and-release fishing, an ever-increasing number of returning fish began to be noticed, with the result that the Rio Grande and Rio Gallegos are now recognized as the premium sea-trout fisheries in the world, with healthy runs of fish at a consistently large average size.

WHEN TO GO

The season starts in early November and finishes in mid-April. While there are usually good concentrations of fish in the rivers throughout this time, the most consistently good fishing, in terms of weather conditions and overall numbers of fish, is probably January to March. It should be remembered that some of the very largest fish seem to return in the earliest months of the season, and that by the end of the season the returning fish are more evenly spread

LEFT Tom McGuane and guide Steve Estela land and release a 25-pounder on the Villa Maria beat of the Rio Grande. Caught on a bomber, this was the largest dry-fly-caught fish of the 1998 season.

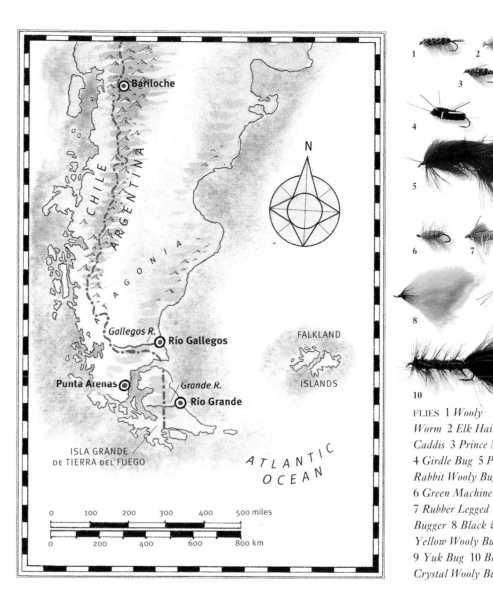

FLIES 1 *Wooly Worm* 2 *Elk Hair Caddis* 3 *Prince Nymph* 4 *Girdle Bug* 5 *Purple Rabbit Wooly Bugger* 6 *Green Machine* 7 *Rubber Legged Wooly Bugger* 8 *Black & Yellow Wooly Bugger* 9 *Yuk Bug* 10 *Black Crystal Wooly Bugger*

throughout the river, which can make for heavier daily bags. Not all fish caught will be fresh from the sea, but sport may be more constant.

TACKLE

RODS: Single-handed rods – 9 ft for 8 or 9 wt line. Double-handed rods – 12–14 ft for 8–11 wt lines.

REELS: Direct-drive reels with good drag systems capable of holding line and 150–200 yards of backing.

LINES: All fly lines from full floater to "Teeny 300" or "deepwater express" lines.

LEADERS: In general, leader weights should not fall below about 10 lb strength.

FLIES: A wide range of flies has proven effective against Argentine sea trout, from Bombers, large Wulff dry flies, and Muddlers fished in clear water conditions, to Zonkers, Wooly Buggers and other streamers fished wet in heavier, colder water. Several more traditional patterns have also proven effective.

The Start of the South

Chile

RODERICK HAIG-BROWN

"Most of the pools in this part of the Quepe are deep and dark, quite narrow and quite short, with a heavy run of water through them. At the head of a pool of this sort the green fly caught me a lovely four-and-a-half-pound brown trout. Soon after that I asked Fonfach to stop and let me work a pool where a narrow, two-hundred-foot fall poured straight down past a solid bank of blooming fuchsia. Another four-pound brown lay just past the foot of the fall and took the fly in a swirl of bronze."

Jacko Edwards is a Santiago newspaperman, a keen trout fisherman and a former member of the Chilean international tuna team. He is a slender, volatile man, a charming and extremely civilized companion. He is a true Chilean, but was born in England while his father was in the diplomatic service there, and he was educated in Paris, returning to Chile when he was seventeen or eighteen. I spent the next month with Jacko, traveling the rivers and lakes of the south, from Temuco to Puerto Montt, and there wasn't a moment of him that I didn't enjoy.

Temuco is a town of some sixty thousand people, a clean and pretty place with some good stores and many things, including fishing tackle, camera film and Scotch whisky, which a tourist cannot always find readily in the south. I had all the tackle I needed; I am not a camera enthusiast and I had no intention of drinking whisky, Scotch or otherwise, in a country that produces a respectable gin, several good brandies, another admirable distillate of the grape called Pisco, and wines that are unequaled except in France. But I record the availability of these commodities out of respect for the good people of Temuco, and to counteract the arrogant assumption that, away from Santiago, shopping facilities in Chile are primitive. They are not. Osorno and Puerto Varas, and for all I know a dozen other places, are as much on the job as Temuco.

Temuco does, I think, still pride itself on being a frontier town – the name of its excellent modern hotel, Hotel de la Frontera, suggests that. It is the start of the south – the vegetation along the nearby rivers confirms that. And it is the heart of the Indian country, the land of the Araucanas, the proud race which never accepted conquest by the Spaniards. I say the heart of their country because Pedro Valdivia, the founder of Chile, is said to have been killed by the Indians on a rock bluff overlooking the Laja right by the Palacio, two hundred miles north of Temuco; because the last great war was fought around Villarica, fifty or sixty miles south; and because I saw more full-blooded Indians near Temuco than anywhere else. But in truth there has been in Chile such a magnificent freedom of intermarriage between the native Indians and the invading whites that it can be said the country is fairly apportioned between invaders and invaded, to the lasting benefit of both.

Jacko had already made arrangements to go fishing. After fourteen-hour days on the Laja and at Maule, they shocked me a little, but we were out of our comfortable beds by 4.30 the next morning and starting from the hotel entrance in a rackety truck by 5.00 am. The truck carried two fair-sized hardwood skiffs, ourselves, two boatmen, a driver and a swamper, whose sole business was to help unload the heavy boats.

We jolted along some fifteen or twenty miles of rough road to a bridge over the Cautin River, backed the truck down as near to the water as possible and slid the

RIGHT *Lago Yelcho is an ancient, deep, glacial lake in southern Chile famous among fishermen for the incoming and outgoing rivers Futaleufú and Yelcho.*

ABOVE *An eagerly awaited streamside* asado *(barbecue) is about to be served up by host John Jenkins of Patagonia Outfitters.*

boats in, not without difficulty. The driver, a keen fisherman himself, wished us good fishing, the truck pulled away and we started out into the stream.

My boatman, Gemán Fonfach, was a very dignified, respectable, middle-aged man, powerfully built and with the obvious confidence of experience. He was reputed to be the best boatman in the Temuco area, an enthusiast for the fly, and himself both a good fisherman and a good fly-tyer. He took me firmly in hand at once, which was reasonable enough, looked over my fly boxes and indicated very pronounced preference for large flies of an olive or yellowish-brown type; his favorite was the Norton, which seems to me a very large stonefly imitation, and after that a big green drake or else the San Pedro streamer, which is winged with long, barred cock's hackles dyed yellow. He would have none of Mac's Gray Ghost, which had done well for us on the Laja, or of a brown shrimp fly that had risen me some good fish. But he did let me use a fly of my own, dressed with green gantron chenille and a mixed polar-bear wing, in a somewhat smaller size than his favorites.

All this interested me very much indeed, because I knew I should be fishing with boatmen through much of Chile and I was at least as anxious to learn about the boatmen themselves as anything else. If one must have a guide, the manner of his guiding is all-important to the day's pleasure. Choice of fly usually does not worry me too much, especially when I am fishing wet, and I make it a rule to fish a boatman's preference rather than my own whenever I reasonably can – it gives him confidence and encourages him to make more important concessions; besides, he may have some special knowledge. Fonfach, as it turned out, had.

He understood at once that I wanted to wade and cast wherever possible, but the first reaches of the Cautin offered little opportunity for this and he handled the boat beautifully through them while I cast into the likely places. We caught one or two small rainbows of a pound or so, then I rolled a good fish at the head of a deep run. "*El flojo,*" Fonfach said. "The lazy one. Brown trout."

The river was easy and swift, over a gravelly bottom and through flat land; it is smaller than the Laja, it does not divide, as the Laja does, into many river-size branches, and the vegetation along its banks is generally richer and greener and stronger; yet the two rivers are somewhat similar and I could well believe in the Cautin's reputation as a great trout stream. But I could sense that Fonfach did not expect a big day. When I rolled a second big brown trout he was obviously surprised to see the fish, and just as obviously was not surprised when the fly came away.

He explained why almost at once: November and December were the river's good months; January and February were too warm; all the big fish were lying deep and disinclined to take, though they would be moving again in

March and April. I checked the river temperature and found it was 69°F (20°C).

As the stream opened up to shallower water Fonfach began to put me out at many favorable places, and I worked them comfortably and happily in the bright sunshine, finding an abundance of bright fourteen- and fifteen-inch rainbows, but nothing of any size. From time to time we passed and repassed Jacko and his boat-man, and it was plain that Jacko, using a light spinning outfit with an assortment of plugs and spinners, was faring much as we were – no better, no worse. So I came to the time and place of my first real fishing lunch in Chile.

I had heard of these magnificent meals, but I was by no means prepared for the formality or the efficiency of the affair. We stopped outside a wide, shallow reach of the river, where there were some fine trees and a heavy growth of bamboo. Almost immediately the two boatmen had a great fire of bamboo and hardwood burning strongly. Four bottles of wine were set in the river to cool. Jacko's boat-man was cleaning and filleting some of the trout we had caught; Fonfach was preparing a long bamboo stake on which he impaled several pounds of mutton, to be barbecued when the fire had died down. It was clear that there was nothing for Jacko and me to do except lie in the shade and take our ease, and that, Jacko assured me, was exactly what we were expected to do.

BELOW *A Zonker.*

"The boatmen will rest afterward," he said. "And for quite long enough. It is noon now. They will not start fishing again until three o'clock at the soonest."

"That's quite a while," I said. "What do they do?"

"Eat all the food and drink all the wine, then sleep. They say it is the bad hour for fish, from twelve till three, and nothing can be caught. But I don't see how they can know, because no one in Chile ever fishes at that time."

There were plates in front of us now, with fillets of trout swimming in black butter, another plate with an excellent salad of lettuce and tomatoes, hot green peppers and French dressing. The wine bottles were open. Fonfach had his meat browning over the fire, potatoes baking in the ashes, water boiling for coffee. I accepted the bad hour and was grateful for it.

Later, when the food was eaten and most of the wine was gone, I suppose I slept for a little. But I was awake at 1.30, listening to the chatter of parakeets in the trees above me. I could see them, none too clearly, against the sky, then suddenly the whole flock took off. They were brilliant green in the sunlight, slender bodies on narrow wings, like arrows, straight and swift in flight. I sat up and saw Jacko asleep on his back, the two boatmen asleep with their blanket ponchos thrown over them. I picked up my rod and stole away to the river.

It was an easy place to wade and I found a good run on the shady side of an island, within fifty yards of the boats. My pale green fly was taken solidly at the

LEFT The view from Isla Monita, a fishing lodge located on Lago Yelcho in a wildly spectacular setting of snowcapped mountains.

BELOW An angler tosses Wooly Buggers for rainbows off the boca of the Rio Paloma.

BELOW *Bamboo forests, monkey-puzzle trees, glaciers, waterfalls, and all sorts of unusual sights may thrill the senses on a float down the Rio Yelcho.*

first cast and the fish ran hard, well down into the backing. Then he jumped and I was surprised to see a silvery rainbow not much larger than those I had been catching in the morning. I netted him and quickly took two others from the run, both excellent fighters and exactly the same size as the first – sixteen inches and one and three-quarter pounds.

I had noticed some very pale green caterpillars on the bushes near where we had lunch and the quick success of my green-bodied fly made me curious, so I cleaned the fish at once. The caterpillars were in them, with a few apancora and another pale green, shield-shaped bug that Fonfach later called the sanfoin or copiala beetle. I understood why my green-bodied fly had taken his fancy.

It turned out that those three fish were the best of the day, though Jacko and I killed twenty-five or thirty between us, all of them over a pound. We ran through some fine-looking water during the afternoon, passed the boats over an irrigation dam a few miles above Temuco, and from there to the outskirts of the town itself saw a dozen places that must hold big trout. I was hopeful of the good hour between sunset and dark, but we came to the end of the run before that – among a multitude of the good citizens of Temuco swimming in their warm stream and with a welcome from the local fishing club, whose boats Fonfach had borrowed for us.

It was, I suppose, a disappointing day, because the Cautin has a considerable reputation for big fish. But Fonfach assured me the reputation is well deserved; in November and December one can expect an average weight of two and a quarter pounds on most days, with several fish of between four and six pounds. I have little doubt he is right because a random sample of our catch that day proved to be all fish in their second or third year, none had spawned and most were immature. A fourth-year fish would certainly be over two pounds and could be very much larger.

Our next day's fishing was in the Quepe, some twenty miles south of the Cautin and a very different stream. The Quepe is smaller than the Cautin, with brownish, rushing water, and it twists and turns its way between canyon-like clay banks that are often a hundred and fifty or two hundred feet high.

We started out cheerfully in the truck with the boats at some much too early hour, and pounded five or six miles over bad roads before discovering we had forgotten the lunch. Clearly the truck had to go back for it, and Jacko and I decided to walk until it caught up with us again. We were in rolling, rather dry country with a few primitive-looking thatched Indian huts scattered through it. Most of the huts had gardens, whose main crop seemed to be healthy-looking potatoes. We met many Indian women walking toward the town, some young, some old, all walking well and

ABOVE *A Bunny Leech*.

handsomely dressed in flowered dresses and dark blue capes of blanket-like material, often lined with red. They wore impressively heavy silver ornaments on their breasts, hinged and pieced, decorated with crosses and coins and sometimes beads. The workmanship was quite remarkable and the designs varied considerably; I felt they must have some significance, but our happy truck-driver insisted they were simply decoration. I asked Jacko why we saw only women. "Only the women work," he said. "They are going to market to sell the stuff we have seen in the carts."

Our truck caught up to us, we climbed aboard and went on again. The driver was regretful he could not fish with us. The Quepe was his favorite river and we would surely have great sport. As we launched the boats he gave me, with Fonfach's approval, two big dark streamer flies he had tied himself on No. 2 hooks, each with a smaller hook trailing behind it. They were, he assured me, the best possible medicine for the river, and as Fonfach seemed to agree I started out with the smaller one, a mixture of black and barred hackles.

The Quepe seemed to take us into herself almost immediately and we were lost between the high banks as though in a forest. The banks themselves were quite wonderful, dripping with fuchsia in full bloom, matted with bamboo, patterned with some lovely yellow flower almost like a pansy. Acacias and weeping willows and other handsome trees grew wherever there was root-hold. The enormous leaves of the giant gunnera, often five or six feet across, stood out as a perpetual reminder of strangeness. And the river itself butted against the base of its banks,

ABOVE *The Rio Simpson is one of the finest dry-fly rivers in Chile. You can spot the fish in the clear water when the sun is high, or fish to their rise forms in the evening.*

twisted round right-angled corners and broke white against log jams, in test after formidable test of Fonfach's skill with the boat. It was far from being the swiftest or fiercest of the boat rivers I saw in Chile, but in many ways it was the tightest and trickiest to work and I began to appreciate the skill and boldness that Chilean boatmen have.

It was a cloudy day and considerably cooler than any other day I had seen in Chile. The river temperature where we started in was only 60°F (15°C) and I began to believe we should have a good day. We did. By lunchtime I had five fish of over two and a half pounds, the biggest a rainbow of just under four pounds, all of them caught on the truck-driver's black streamer. There was a shower of rain at lunchtime, short and swift and violent, and when we began fishing again I noticed that fish were coming short to the streamer, so I changed again to my green fly – the only smallish fly I had that Fonfach would approve.

Most of the pools in this part of the Quepe are deep and dark, quite narrow and quite short, with a heavy run of water through them. At the head of a pool of this sort the green fly caught me a lovely four-and-a-half pound brown trout. Soon after that I asked Fonfach to stop and let me work a pool where a narrow, two-hundred-foot fall poured straight down past a solid bank of blooming fuchsia. Another four-pound brown lay just past the foot of the fall and took the fly in a swirl of bronze. Neither of these fish rated Fonfach's contemptuous nick-name, El Flojo, but later in the day, in a wider pool, I hooked a three-pound brown that walked clear across the current on his tail, for all the world like a marlin. I glanced at Fonfach and asked him, "El Flojo?" He laughed and shook his head. "Not always."

The truck met us at dusk by a bridge far down the river. I had returned over twenty fish, but Fonfach had kept smaller fish than I wanted and there were seventeen in the boat when we landed, eleven of them between two and a half and four and a half pounds. Jacko had a similar catch on spoon and flatfish though his best fish, to my surprise, was a three-pounder. As nearly as I could judge from the reactions of the boatmen and the truck-driver and his helpers, the catch was a good one for the river at any time. Scale readings confirmed this, as the big brown trout were five-year-olds that had spawned previously and the best rainbow, a fish of three and three-quarter pounds, had spawned at three years. I thought it a fine day, though I should have been content to fish only a quarter of the distance in the same length of time. We had passed dozens of wonderful places without fishing them, and it seemed to me we had come to the best water very late in the day.

No small part of the pleasure of a Chilean day like this is in the sharp contrast between the wildness of the river and its surroundings and the luxury of the evening at the hotel. By 10.30 we had changed our clothes, had a quiet drink in the bar and were sitting down to dinner in the big, graceful dining room of the Frontera. There was good food, well served, and good wine to go with it. A small orchestra played South American music at the far end of the room. Well-dressed men and handsome women sat at the other tables around the room; faded blue denims and Hawaiian sports shirts, weather-ravaged faces and casual manners simply were not to be seen. At 7.00 or 7.30 all this would have been an intolerable nuisance, to be avoided by any sensible fisherman. But at 10.30 or 11.00, the day is over, the last hour has been fished, daylight is exhausted. It is a perfect time to relax, to enjoy an appetite and feel thoroughly civilized.

BELOW *The Futaleufú, which flows into Lago Yelcho, is a large river, and glacial melt gives it a beautiful turquoise color.*

CHILE: FACTFILE

BACKGROUND

Chile is one of the world's most varied countries, covering 2,000 miles from north to south. It encompasses one of the driest deserts in the world, the beautiful Lake District, the western hemisphere's oldest vineyards, and the Patagonian region. In southern Chile the huge mountains, glaciers and fjords produce countless lakes and rivers, which harbour several species of trout and salmon.

Situated in the southern hemisphere, Chile is a great getaway location during the northern hemisphere's winter, and home to a hospitable people – under the code of the pilgrim, Patagonian *estancia* owners used to provide free meals and shelter for the wayfarer, a practice that has evolved into a cultural tradition.

Some of the best fly-fishing is found in Chilean Patagonia, a region with many similarities to the western USA and the North American Pacific coast. Innumerable lakes and rivers, some of them huge, are filled with predominantly brown trout, rainbows and a few brook trout.

Aquaculture is a rapidly growing industry, with many different species of fish being raised commercially. Unfortunately winter storms have caused flooding and many of these exotic species have escaped and spawned in the rivers, creating new runs of non-indigenous fish. It is still unclear if any of these runs will establish themselves into permanent spawning migrations.

Chile has had a strong fly-fishing heritage for the last 50–70 years. Roderick Haig-Brown wrote about his fishing experiences there in the 1950s in his classic *Fisherman's Winter*, an excellent choice of reading for anyone preparing a trip. The scenic beauty and the possibilities of adventure make the country an exciting option for the travelling angler.

WHEN TO GO

The season starts in November and finishes in April, although many of the rivers may be running high and coloured in the early weeks. At practically

LEFT A typical brown trout from the Rio Simpson. Note the purple patch on the gill plate.

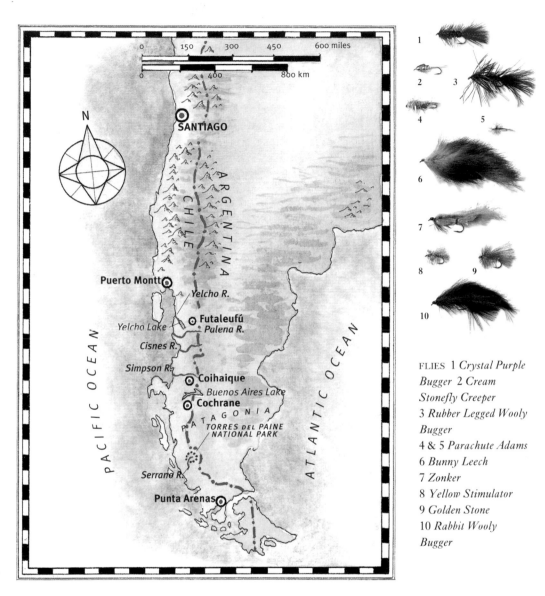

FLIES 1 *Crystal Purple Bugger* 2 *Cream Stonefly Creeper* 3 *Rubber Legged Wooly Bugger* 4 & 5 *Parachute Adams* 6 *Bunny Leech* 7 *Zonker* 8 *Yellow Stimulator* 9 *Golden Stone* 10 *Rabbit Wooly Bugger*

any other time in the season the fishing will be more consistent.

TACKLE

RODS: Single-handed 9 ft rods for 5–6 wt line and a 7–8 wt line.

REELS: Direct-drive reels with a good drag system.

LINES: A full complement is desirable: weight-forward floating, sink-tip and a couple of full sinking lines of different densities. The Teeny series and the Rio windcutters are popular choices.

LEADERS: Floating lines – leader of 5–8 lb test tippet. Sinking lines – 6–9 ft with 8–15 lb tippet.

FLIES: Classic dry-fly patterns: Adams, Wulff, Humpy, Elk Hair Caddis, Irresistibles, Hoppers and Beetles. For wet flies it is hard to beat the Olive or Black Wooly Bugger; also Hare's Ears and Pheasant Tail Nymphs. In the lakes, Dragonfly or Damselfly (wet and dry) where naturals are present.

The Dreadnaught Pool

New Zealand

Zane Grey

"The sun had set as I waded in again. A shimmering ethereal light moved over the pool. The reflection of the huge bluff resembled a battleship more than the bluff itself. Clear and black-purple rose the mountain range, and golden clouds grew more deeply gold. The river roared above and below, deep-toned and full of melody. A cool breeze drifted down from upstream. I cast over all the water I had previously covered without raising a fish. Farther out and down I saw trout rising, curling dark tails out of the gold gleam on the water."

"This pool here is called Dreadnaught," said [the Maori guide] Hoka, pointing to a huge steep bluff strikingly like the shape of a dismantled man-of-war. It stood up all alone. The surrounding banks were low and green. After one glance, I gave my attention to picking my steps among the boulders, while Hoka kept on talking. "My people once fought battles here. They had a *pa* on top of this bluff. I'll show you graves that are wearing away. The skulls roll down into the river. Yes, my people, the Maoris, were great fighters. They stood up face to face, and gave blow for blow, like men."

The lower and larger end of that pool grew fascinating to me. Under the opposite bank the water looked deep and dark. A few amber-colored rocks showed at the closer edge of the current. It shoaled toward the wide part, with here and there a golden boulder gleaming far under the water. What a wonderful pool!

I could see now how such a pool might reward a skillful far-casting angler, when the rainbows were running. After a long climb up rapids, what a pool to rest in! There might even be a trout resting there then. So I picked up my rod and strode down to the river.

A clean sand bar ran out thirty yards or more, shelving into deep green water. Here a gliding swirling current moved off to the center of the pool, and turned toward the glancing incline at the head of the narrow rapid. The second and heavier current worked farther across. By wading to the limit I imagined I might cast to the edge of that bed water. I meant to go leisurely and try the closer current first. It was my kind of a place. It kept growing upon me. I waded in to my knees, and cast half across this nearer current. My big fly sank and glided on. I followed it with my eye, and then gave it a slight jerky movement. Darker it became, and passed on out of my sight, where the light on the water made it impossible for me to see. I had scarcely forty feet of line out. It straightened below me, and then I whipped it back and cast again, taking a step or two farther on the sand bar.

My line curved and straightened. Mechanically I pulled a yard or so off my reel, then drew perhaps twice as much back, holding it in loops in my left hand. Then I cast again, letting all the loose line go. It swept out, unrolled and alighted straight, with the fly striking gently. Was that not a fine cast? I felt gratified. "Pretty poor, I don't think," I soliloquized, and stole a glance upriver to see if the Captain had observed my beautiful cast. Apparently he did not know I was on the river. Then I looked quickly back at my fly.

It sank just at the edge of the light place on the water. I lost sight of it, but knew about where it floated. Suddenly right where I was looking on this glancing sunlit pool came a deep angry swirl. Simultaneously with this came a swift powerful pull, which ripped the line out of my left hand, and then jerked my rod down straight.

"Zee-eee!" shrieked my reel.

Then the water burst white, and a huge trout leaped in spasmodic action. He shot up, curved and black, his great jaws wide and sharp. I saw his spread tail quivering. Down he thumped, making splash and spray.

Then I seemed to do many things at once. I drew my rod up, despite the strain upon it; I backed toward the shore; I reeled frantically, for the trout ran upstream; I yelled for Morton and then for Captain Mitchell.

"Doc, he's a wolloper!" yelled the Captain.

"Oh, biggest trout I ever saw!" I returned wildly.

Once out of the water I ran up the beach toward Captain Mitchell, who was wading to meet me. I got even with my fish, and regained all but part of the bag in my line. What a weight! I could scarcely hold the six-ounce rod erect. The tip bent far over, and wagged like a buggy whip.

"Look out when he turns!" called Mitchell.

When the fish struck the swift current, he leaped right before me. I saw him with vivid distinctness – the largest trout that I ever saw on line of mine – a dark bronze-backed and rose-sided male, terribly instinct with the ferocity and strength of self-preservation; black-spotted, big-finned, hook-nosed. I heard the heavy shuffle as he shook himself. Then he tumbled back.

ABOVE *Anglers cast to cruising browns on the shores of Lake Wakatipu near Queenstown on South Island.*

78

"Now!" yelled Captain Mitchell, right behind me.

I knew. I was ready. The rainbow turned. Off like an arrow!

"Zee! Zee! Zee!" he took a hundred yards of line.

"Oh Morton! Morton! … *Camera*!" I shouted hoarsely, with every nerve in my body at supreme strain. What would his next jump be? After that run! I was all aquiver. He was as big as my black Marlin. My tight line swept up to the surface as I have seen it sweep with so many fish. "He's coming out!" I yelled for Morton's benefit.

Then out he came magnificently. Straight up six feet, eight feet and over, a regular salmon leap he made, gleaming beautifully in the sun. What a picture! If only Morton got him with the camera I would not mind losing him, as surely I must lose him. Down he splashed. "*Zee!*" whizzed my line.

I heard Morton running over the boulders, and turned to see him making toward his camera. He had not been ready. What an incomparable opportunity lost! I always missed the greatest pictures! My impatience and disappointment vented themselves upon poor Morton, who looked as if he felt as badly as I. Then a hard jerk on my rod turned my gaze frantically back to the pool, just in time to see the great rainbow go down from another grand leap. With that he sheered round to the left, into the center of the wide swirl. I strode rapidly down the beach and into the water, winding my reel as fast as possible. How hard to hold that tip up and yet to recover line! My left arm ached, my right arm shook; for that matter, my legs shook also. I was hot and cold by turns. My throat seemed as tight as my line. Dry-mouthed, clogged in my lungs, with breast heaving, I strained every faculty to do what was right. Who ever said a trout could not stir an angler as greatly as a whale?

One sweep he made put my heart in my throat. It was toward the incline in the rapids. If he started down! But he ended with a leap, head upstream, and when he soused back he took another run, closer inshore toward me. Here I had to reel like a human windlass.

He was too fast; he got a slack line, and to my dismay and panic he jumped on that slack line. My mind whirled, and the climax of my emotions hung upon that moment. Suddenly, tight jerked my line again. The hook had held. He was fairly close at hand, in good position, head upriver, and tiring. I waded out on the beach; and though he chugged and tugged and bored he never again got the line out over fifty feet. Sooner or later – it seemed both only a few moments and a long while – I worked him in over the sand bar, where in the crystal water I saw every move of his rose-red body. How I reveled in his beauty! Many times he stuck out his open jaws, cruel beaks, and gaped and snapped and gasped.

At length I slid him out upon the sand, and that moment my vaunted championship of the Oregon steelhead suffered an eclipse. The great Oregon rainbow, transplanted to the snow waters of the Tongariro, was superior in every way to his Oregon cousin, the silver-pink steelhead that had access to the sea. I never looked down upon such a magnificent game fish. No artist could have caught with his brush the shining flecked bronze, the deep red flush from jaw to tail, the amber and pearl. Perforce he would have been content to catch the grand graceful contour of body, the wolf-jawed head, the lines of fins and tail.

He weighed eleven and one-half pounds. I tied him on a string, as I was wont to do with little fish when a boy, and watched him recover and swim about in the clear water.

As if by magic of nature the Dreadnaught Pool had been transformed. The something that was evermore about to happen to me in my fishing had happened there. There! The beautiful pool glimmered, shone, ran swiftly on, magnified in my sight. The sun was westering. It had lost its heat and glare. A shadow lay under the bluff. Only at the lower end did the sunlight make a light on the water, and it had changed. No longer hard to look upon!

I waded in up to my knees and began to cast with short line, gradually lengthening it, but now not leisurely, contentedly, dreamily! My nerves were as keen as the edge of a blade. Alert, quick, restrained, with all latent powers ready for instant demand, I watched my line sweep out and unroll, my leader straighten, and the big dark fly alight. What singularly pleasant sensations attended the whole procedure!

I knew I would raise another rainbow trout. That was the urge, wherefore the pool held more thrill and delight and stir for me. On the fifth cast, when the line in its sweep downstream had reached its limit, I had a strong vibrating strike. Like the first trout, this one hooked himself; and on his run he showed in a fine jump – a fish scarcely half as large as my first one. He ran out of the best fishing water, and eventually came over the sand bar, where I soon landed him, a white-and-rose fish, plump and solid, in the very best condition.

"Fresh-run trout," said Hoka. "They've just come up from the lake."

"By gad! then the run is on," returned Captain Mitchell with satisfaction.

RIGHT *A small spring creek winds its way down to meet the Eglinton River along the road to Milford Sound, South Island. This valley is probably one of the most beautiful in the world.*

This second fish weighed five and three-quarter pounds. He surely had all
the strength of an eight-pound steelhead in his compact colorful body.

"Cap, make a few casts with my rod while I rest and hug the fire," I said.
"That water has ice beaten a mile."

"Not on your life," replied the Captain warmly. "I've a hunch it's
your day. Wade in; every moment now is precious."

So I found myself out again on the sand bar, casting and recasting, gradually
wading out until I was over my hips and could go no farther. At that I drew my
breath sharply when I looked down. How deceiving that water! Another step would
have carried me over my head. If the bottom had not been sandy I would not have
dared trust myself there, for the edge of the current just caught me and tried to
move me off balance; but I was not to be caught unawares.

Sunlight still lay on the pool, yet cool and dark now, and waning. I fished the

ABOVE *A stealthy approach is critical in outwitting a feeding brown in the back eddy against a granite wall on this Southland stream.*

OPPOSITE ABOVE *Fish on! Well done, lads. A #14 Coch-Y-Bonddu strikes again on the Motueka River.*

part of the pool where I had raised the two trout. It brought no rise. Then I essayed to reach across the gentler current, across the narrow dark still aisle beyond, to the edge of the strong current, sweeping out from the bluff. It was a long cast for me, with a heavy fly, eighty feet or more. How the amber water, the pale-green shadowy depths, the changing lights under the surface seemed to call to me, to assure me, to haunt with magical portent!

Apparently without effort, I cast my fly exactly where I wanted to. The current hungrily seized it, and as it floated out of my sight I gave my rod a gentle motion. Halfway between the cast and where the line would have straightened out before me, a rainbow gave a heavy and irresistible lunge. It was a strike that outdid my first. It almost unbalanced me. It dragged hard on the line I clutched in my left hand. I was as quick as the fish and let go just as he hooked himself. Then followed a run the like of which I did not deem possible for any fish short of a salmon or a Marlin. He took all my line except a quarter of an inch left on the spool. That brought him to the shallow water way across where the right-hand channel went down. He did not want that. Luckily for me, he turned to the left and rounded the lower edge of the pool. Here I got line back. Next he rushed across toward the head of the rapid. I could do nothing but hold on and pray.

Twenty yards above the smooth glancing incline he sprang aloft in so prodigious a leap that my usual ready shout of delight froze in my throat. Like a deer, in long bounds he covered the water, how far I dared not believe. The last rays of the setting sun flashed on this fish, showing it to be heavy and round and deep, of a wonderful pearly white tinted with pink. It had a small head which resembled that of a salmon. I had hooked a big female rainbow, fresh run from old Taupo, and if I had not known before that I had a battle on my hands, I knew it on sight of the fish. Singularly indeed the females of these great rainbow trout are the hardest and fiercest fighters.

Fearing the swift water at the head of the rapid, I turned and plunged pellmell out to the beach and along it, holding my rod up as high as I could. I did not save any line, but I did not lose any, either. I ran clear to the end of the sandy beach where it verged on the boulders. A few paces farther on roared the river.

Then with a throbbing heart and indescribable feelings I faced the pool. There were one hundred and twenty-five yards of line out. The trout hung just above the rapid and there bored deep, to come up and thump on the surface. Inch by inch I lost line. She had her head upstream but the current was drawing her toward the incline. I became desperate. Once over that fall she would escape. The old situation presented itself – break the fish off or hold it. Inch by inch she tugged the line off my reel. With all that line off and most of it out of the water in plain sight, tight as a banjo string, I appeared to be at an overwhelming disadvantage. So I grasped the line in my left hand and held it. My six-ounce rod bowed and bent, then straightened and pointed. I felt its quivering vibration and I heard the slight singing of the tight line.

So there I held this stubborn female rainbow. Any part of my tackle or all of it might break, but not my spirit. How terribly hard it was not to weaken! Not to trust to luck! Not to release that tremendous strain!

The first few seconds were almost unendurable. They seemed an age. When would line or leader give way or the hook tear out? But nothing broke. I could hold the wonderful trout. Then as the moments passed I lost that tense agony of apprehension. I gained confidence. Unless the fish wheeled to race for the fall I would win. The chances were against such a move. Her head was up current, held by that rigid line. Soon the tremendous strain told. The rainbow came up, swirled and pounded and threshed on the surface. There was a time when all old fears returned and augmented;

BELOW *This angler is standing on a big rock – a few more feet and he would be up to his shoulders. The waters of New Zealand are incredibly clear and deceiving.*

but just as I was about to despair, the tension on rod and line relaxed. The trout swirled under and made upstream. This move I signaled with a shout, which was certainly echoed by my comrades, all lined up behind me, excited and gay and admonishing.

I walked down the beach, winding my reel fast, yet keeping the line taut. Thus I advanced fully a hundred yards. When I felt the enameled silk come to my fingers, to slip on the reel, I gave another shout. Then again I backed up the beach, pulling the trout, though not too hard. At last she got into the slack shallow water over the wide sand bar.

ABOVE *A Rat-faced MacDougall.*

Here began another phase of the fight, surely an anxious and grim one for me, with every move of that gorgeous fish as plain as if she had been in the air. What a dogged stubborn almost unbeatable fish on such tackle! Yet that light tackle was just the splendid thing for such a fight. Fair to the fish and calling to all I possessed of skill and judgment! It required endurance, too, for I had begun to tire. My left arm had a cramp and my winding hand was numb.

The fish made short hard runs into the deeper water, yet each run I stopped eventually. Then they gave place to the thumping on the surface, the swirling breaks, the churning rolls, and the bulldog tug, tug, tug. The fight had long surpassed any I had ever had with a small fish. Even that of the ten-pound steelhead I hooked once in wild Deer Creek, Washington! So strong and unconquerable was this rainbow that I was fully a quarter of an hour working her into the shallower part of the bar. Every time the deep silvery side flashed, I almost had heart-failure. This fish would go heavier than the eleven-and-a-half-pound male. I had long felt that in the line, in the rod; and now I saw it. There was a remarkable zest in this part of the contest.

"Work that plugger in close where the water is shallower," advised Captain Mitchell.

Indeed, I had wanted and tried to do that, for the twisting rolling fish might any instant tear out the hook. I held harder now, pulled harder. Many times I led or drew or dragged the trout close to shore, and each time saw the gleaming silver-and-pink shape plunge back into deeper water.

The little rod wore tenaciously on the rainbow, growing stronger, bending less, drawing easier.

After what seemed an interminable period there in this foot-deep water the battle ended abruptly with the bend of the rod drawing the fish head on to the wet sand. Captain Mitchell had waded in back of my quarry, suddenly to lean down and slide her far up on the beach.

"What a bally fine trout!" burst out Morton. "Look at it! Deep, fat, thick. It'll weigh fourteen."

"Oh no," I gasped, working over my numb and aching arms and hands.

"By gad! that's a wonderful trout!" added the Captain, most enthusiastically. "Why, it's like a salmon!"

Certainly I had never seen anything so beautiful in color, so magnificent in contour. It was mother-of-pearl tinged with exquisite pink. The dots were scarcely discernible, and the fullness of swelling graceful curve seemed to outdo nature itself. How the small thoroughbred salmon-like head

ABOVE *New Zealand's streams are as colorful as an artist's palette. This is a back-country stream in the Springs Junction area of South Island.*

contrasted with the huge iron-jawed fierce-eyed head of the male I had caught first! It was strange to see the broader tail of the female, the thicker mass of muscled body, the larger fins. Nature had endowed this progenitor of the species, at least for the spawning season, with greater strength, speed, endurance, spirit and life.

"Eleven pounds, three-quarters!" presently sang out the Captain. "I missed it a couple of pounds. ... Some rainbow, old man. Get in there and grab another."

"Won't you have a try with my rod?" I replied. "I'm darn near froze to death. Besides I want to put this one on a string with the others and watch them."

He was obdurate, so I went back into the water; and before I knew what was happening, almost, I had fastened to another trout. It did not have the great dragging weight of the other two, but it gave me a deep boring fight and deceived me utterly as to size. When landed, this, my fourth trout, weighed six and three-quarters, another female, fresh run from the lake, and a fine rainbow in hue.

"Make it five, Doc. This is your day. Anything can happen now. Get out your line," declared Mitchell, glowing of face.

The sun had set as I waded in again. A shimmering ethereal light moved over the pool. The reflection of the huge bluff resembled a battleship more than the bluff itself. Clear and black-purple rose the mountain range, and golden clouds grew more deeply gold. The river roared above and below, deep-toned and full of melody. A cool breeze drifted down from upstream.

I cast over all the water I had previously covered without raising a fish. Farther out and down I saw trout rising, curling dark tails out of the gold gleam on the water. I waded a foot farther than ever and made a cast, another, recovered line, then spent all the strength I had left in a cast that covered the current leading to the rising trout. I achieved it. The fly disappeared, my line glided on and on, suddenly to stretch like a whipcord and go zipping out of my left hand. Fast and hard!

What a wonderful thrill ran up and down my back, all over me!

"Ho! Ho! ... Boys, I've hung another!" I bawled out, in stentorian voice. "Say, but he's taking line! ... Oh, look at him jump! ... Oh, two! ... Oh, three! ... Four, by gosh! ... Oh, Morton, if we only had some sunlight! What a flying leapfrog this trout is! ... *Five*!"

The last jump was splendid, with a high parabolic curve, and a slick cutting back into the water. This rainbow, too, was big, fast, strong and fierce. But the fish did everything that should not have been done and I did everything right. Fisherman's luck! Beached and weighed before my cheering companions: nine and one-half pounds; another silvery rosy female rainbow, thick and deep and wide!

ABOVE *My biggest brown to date ... a little under 9 lb. I spotted him while eating lunch on a gravel bar next to a main highway.*

LEFT *A Czech Shrimp.*

LEFT *A scene of jubilation between friends over a good fish in the net.*

NEW ZEALAND: FACTFILE

BACKGROUND

Zane Grey called New Zealand an "Angler's El Dorado". He was more enamoured of the big game fishing he found in Mercury Bay and the Bay of Islands, but his steelheading experiences back in the USA eventually led him to try the Tongariro River and Lake Taupo. The stories he wrote about them have fuelled the imagination of fishermen since.

If Taupo and the Tongariro are synonymous with giant lake-run rainbows, South Island is justly famous for its brown trout. The remote rivers of the south-west coast are ideally suited to the "stalking" method of fishing which for many epitomizes fishing in New Zealand. Armed with a handful of dry flies and nymphs and a pair of Polaroid sunglasses, fishermen walk upriver with a local guide, whose trained eyes help them spot the superbly camouflaged quarry. In such clear waters, careful fly presentation is as important as fly choice, and a "lined" fish (scared off by the line or its shadow) is a lost opportunity. Leaders need to be long to try to avoid this eventuality, but even so, many expert fishermen have been humbled by New Zealand trout.

A good day's fishing might consist of, say, 15 fish being spotted and five landed, typically between 4 and 8 lb, with a good possibility of double-figure fish being encountered. New Zealand looks set to remain the world's finest freshwater trout location.

WHEN TO GO

With the southern hemisphere summer, the season starts in October and goes on until April. Many New Zealanders take their summer holidays after Christmas, and January is perhaps the busiest time on the rivers. On North Island around Taupo, fishing is best in the winter months (April to August) when the rainbows leave the lake to spawn in the rivers that flow into it.

TACKLE

RODS: Single-handed 9–11 ft rods for 4, 5 and 7 wt lines.
REELS: Direct-drive reels, with good drag systems and capacity for 100 yards of backing.

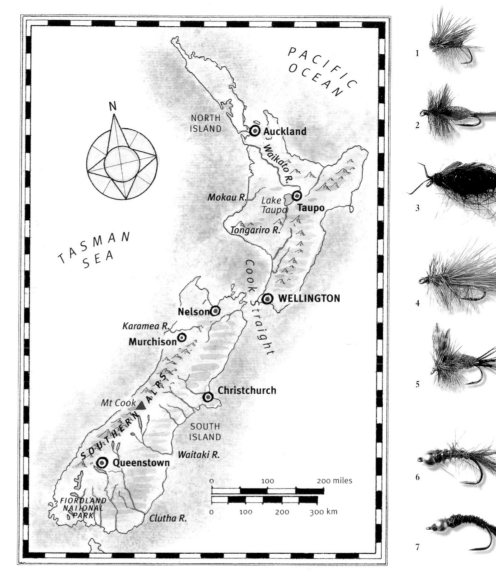

LINES: Most fishing will be with floating lines, but sink-tips are useful.

LEADERS: Take plenty of spools between 3 lb and 6 lb as tippet changes may be frequent.

FLIES: Dry flies – Royal Wulff, Humpy, Adams, Irresistible and Caddis. Nymphs – Pheasant Tail and Hare's Ear.

FLIES 1 *Elk Hair Caddis* 2 *Rat-faced McDougall* 3 *Stonefly Nymph* 4 *Yellow Stimulator* 5 *Adams Irresistible* 6 *Gold Head Hare's Ear Nymph* 7 *Gold Head Pheasant Tail Nymph* 8 *Sawyer's Pheasant Tail Nymph* 9 *Hi-Float Beetle* 10 *Czech Shrimp*

Salmon

I Know a Good Place

Alaska

CLIVE GAMMON

"And now, though this is my seventh morning on the Karluk, the fly rod shakes in my hand as I scramble up the loose pebbles to watch the army that's surging into the Karluk's mouth – the day's new wave of coho salmon streams out of the Pacific on the turn of the tide, thousands of bright-struck fish leaping, cavorting like circus clowns."

ABOVE *A Sculpin.*

ABOVE LEFT *Although brown bears are a fairly common sight in Alaska, up close and personal they never fail to command a healthy respect.*

Sometime in the mid-nineteenth century, when the Oregon Territory was still in dispute between Great Britain and the USA, a Royal Commission headed out from London to inspect the damn place, see if it was worth having. It reported back to Parliament in a strongly negative style, the nobleman who was its chairman having been disgusted to discover that the salmon in the Columbia River did not rise to the fly like those of the Tweed. This, conceivably, altered the history of North America. It was also a slander on noble fish, as you will see.

Over the Shelikof Strait the morning sky had the iridescent sheen of the shell of a freshly shucked oyster, steel gray suffused with pink and blue lights that took fire on the snows of the Valley of Ten Thousand Smokes and on Mount Katmai,

ABOVE *The first flight out in the morning from Enchanted Lake Lodge in Katmai National Park, south of Iliamna Lake on the Aleutian Peninsula.*

a 6,700-foot-high volcano forty-five miles away on mainland Alaska.

The sea was an oyster shell, too, blue with rose highlights, calm, barely moving until it broke lazily against the monolithic cliff of Tanglefoot, stirring the kelp, pushing by Mary's Creek until the water swirling out of the Karluk River checked and roiled it. This was slack tide, with the water as idle as the fur seals riding the little swells, immobile as the three bald eagles settled on a stony spit in the river.

The Karluk itself, on the west coast of Kodiak Island in the Gulf of Alaska, looked barren; empty, translucent water slid fast over gray stones until it met the Shelikof in an acre or two of confused chop. On a ridge

95

above, I watched the water for a sign that the ocean was starting to bully its way in again. The seals had vanished, the eagles taken to the air before my senses picked up the change and the daily miracles that would come with it, foreshadowed now by a fretting of the calm water and the silver reflection in it, like the sun catching the shields of an ancient army's vanguard.

And now, though this is my seventh morning on the Karluk, the fly rod shakes in my hand as I scramble up the loose pebbles to watch the army that's surging into the Karluk's mouth – the day's new wave of coho salmon streams out of the Pacific on the turn of the tide, thousands of bright-struck fish leaping, cavorting like circus clowns.

Stripping line as I go, slithering down the stones, I wade clumsily out into the river, launch the garish green-and-purple streamer fly, flashy with tinsel, into the thick of them. My right hand, gripping the rod butt, is wrapped with half a dozen Band-Aids covering cuts of a week's worth of salmon battles. The past seven days have seen this fly rod bend into more than one hundred cohos. Still, I tremble. I am in the finest salmon river in the world, no matter what the people in the rustic lodges along Canada's Restigouche or the tweedy inns on Scotland's Tay or Spey or Dee might think. The Karluk is salmon fishing as known in heaven.

◆

The great fly-fisherman G.E.M. Skues, father of modern nymph-fishing, once unbent enough to write a little fiction concerning the late Mr Castwell, a somewhat bumptious dry-fly purist who, as he thought, had ended up in heaven and been provided with a perfect streamside cottage, the finest tackle and an attendant water keeper. And perfect trout fishing, it seemed, until Mr Castwell began to grow uneasy after catching fish after splendid fish from the same spot. Skues concludes his tale with this bit of dialogue:

"How long is this confounded rise going to last?" inquired Mr Castwell. "I suppose it will stop soon?"

"No, sir," said the keeper.

"What, isn't there a slack hour in the afternoon?"

"No afternoon, sir."

"What? Then what about the evening rise?"

"No evening rise, sir," said the keeper.

"Well, I shall knock off now. I must have had about thirty brace from that corner."

"Beg pardon, sir, but his Holiness would not like that."

"What?" said Mr Castwell. "Mayn't I even stop at night?"

"No night here, sir," said the keeper.

OPPOSITE *The action is often continuous and frenzied when the fresh silver salmon are in. Susan Rockrise lands one of the 79 she caught during her week in Alaska.*

"Then do you mean I have to go on catching these damned two-and-a-half-pounders at this corner for ever and ever?"

The keeper nodded.

"Hell!" said Mr Castwell.

"Yes," said his keeper.

Mr Castwell's hell, though, was confinement to a corner. There was no infinite variety of flies, of techniques, of locations as there was on the Karluk. Nevertheless, the reports of the spectacular fishing over the past year or two had seemed to suggest a kind of drawback that might best be summarized as the Chocolate Factory Syndrome. It's said that chocolate factories have no pilfering problem because employees are free to eat all they want. After a couple of days few of them retain a taste for sweets. Could salmon, then, turn out to be like chocolate? Was it possible to fish until success became satiety?

Journeying to Alaska in midsummer, that seemed unlikely. No fishing could be that good. There would be someone, you could bet your chest waders, who'd greet you at camp with such time-honored words as, "You should have been here last week." And, indeed, during a stopover at Anchorage, there came a foretaste of such a put-down.

That was in Northwest Outfitter's, the city's major tackle store, aglitter with trays of salmon flies. The sales clerk was confidently buoyant about the patterns, as such men always are – the Polar Shrimps, the Skykomish Sunrises, the Bosses, the Skunks. "Figure on one fly for every hour you fish," he said alarmingly, scooping up a dozen Purple Fishairs with Mylar. "You'll want a box for all these and …"

"Did you hear how the silvers are running?" I interrupted him – cohos are often called silvers.

"And you'll need something in green and orange," he said.

The silvers, he was reminded. "Uh, I didn't get word yet," he said offhandedly.

From a tackle salesman, this was the equivalent of a cynical laugh, an indication that the fish were still offshore. I got the same message at the departure lounge for Kodiak, where people were lugging rod cases around as they do garment bags in other airports. "Early for silvers," a rod-bearer said to me. "Where are you heading?" I told him the Karluk. He'd never heard of it.

I needn't have worried. The next morning, forty-five minutes after the light

LEFT *When I called out to Brian O'Keefe that there was a bear right on the bank behind him, he thought I was kidding.*

airplane headed out of Kodiak, over Women's Bay and across the hills and tundra, I looked down on to the thread of the Karluk as it broadened into a lagoon, down on to fish erupting everywhere on its placid surface. Hello, chocolate factory, I said to myself as we landed.

And a factory, it turned out, where there was no need to report for work unconscionably early. The lagoon fish, well, they were sort of semipermanent residents, said Robin Sikes, the elderly Alaskan (elderly at twenty-eight, that's to say, in a state where twenty-six is the median age) who greeted the group of which I was now one. Better to breakfast at leisure, wait for fresh fish to run in from the sea on the tide and enjoy the balmy summer's morning with the temperature in the sixties.

So there was time to make acquaintance with the other anglers in my charter: Drs Hamada, Habu, Hatasaka and Inouye and Mr Okazaki, all from northern

California, all but one dentists; more California dentists, Drs Cosca, Wagner and Angel, with his son Jacob; and the odd men out, Mr Channing, a physical therapist, once a trainer with the 49ers, Mr Sopwith from his Sacramento rice farm, and Mr Lidner and Mr Miley, retirees.

Later they would become Teds, Stans and Leos, et al. Now, as they assembled their gear on the grassy slope in front of the lodge, they divided neatly into two groups – the fly-fishers and the men with, well, the hardware, the spinning gear, the

BELOW *Bus Bergman about to net a big char for his wife Lydia on a float down the Kanektok River.*

heavy spoons. I was no fishing snob, I told myself, but I knew which group I would go to if it came to an emergency root-canal job during the week.

We strolled down to the river together to clock in. Salmon were breaking everywhere in the lower pools, and before I'd even made a first cast I could see one of the spin fishermen with his rod bent into a fish. I took my time, made a short throw or two to get the feel of a new graphite rod, then put out a long cast at the classic angle, across and downstream. The Skykomish Sunrise must have swung by a whole school of leaping fish.

An hour later the silvers were still passing it by, as they did the Purple Fishair I substituted later, and later again the Polar Shrimp. There was a moving belt of salmon, but I hadn't sampled one; nor, so far as I could judge, had the other fly-fishermen. Mortifyingly, the spinning rods were enjoying heavy action. Jacob,

BELOW *Early morning fog greets the first anglers of the day at a wilderness camp on Lake Kagati.*

ABOVE *Hutch, a Bristol Bay Lodge guide, in his mouse-decorated hat. Mouse flies are very effective for rainbow trout.*

eleven years old, was just about keeping his foothold on the pebble bank as a thick-bodied silver, fifteen pounds maybe, tried surging for the volcanoes on the far side of the strait.

When it was clear the run had ended for the morning, I walked back with Jacob to the lodge.

"He was kind of big," Jacob said. "I couldn't reel him in. I thought he was going to win."

"Oh, really," I said.

"I was kind of relieved when I had him on the shore."

"Oh, you landed him, then," I said.

"I wanted to keep him," said Jacob. "Very much. But, see, there's an Eskimo legend that if you kiss the first fish you catch and then you throw it back, it tells its buddies and you can catch more fish."

"And did you kiss it?" I asked Jacob.

"Yeah," he said.

I told him that was terrific as I glanced at the fat spoon now clipped to the keeper-ring on his spinning rod. I tried to smile, but I'm fairly certain it came out like one of those tortured Humphrey Bogart grimaces.

Sikes had said there was a good chance of taking salmon that afternoon in the big lagoon higher up on the Karluk, but the prospect of blind casting into the deep holes up there was unappealing to one nurtured in the white turbulence of northern Atlantic rivers. So I hiked yet farther upstream where the Karluk became a river again.

ABOVE *A Sculpin.*

And a different river, the obverse of the tidal water downstream through which the bright battalions of cohos from the sea had poured in the morning. This was a battlefield in its hideous aftermath. Salmon, dead and dying, leprously white, patchworked in virulent yellows and reds, lolled and drifted in the slack water close to the banks. Fish, sockeyes and humpbacks, that had spawned, and were now spent, finished. And hanging on the flanks of this broken salmon army were river guerillas, Dolly Varden char, pink flecked on their sides, predacious, vicious-hitting, in character absurdly unlike Dickens's delicate heroine of *Barnaby Rudge*, for whose pink-spotted gown the species is named. They gobbled now on the profusion of ripe salmon eggs that dribbled from the stony redds, as four weeks later they would gobble salmon fry. They gobbled also any small bright fly I threw at them, like Mr Castwell's trout, two- and three-pounders hitting on every cast. I had released maybe thirty of them, and I was ready to admit that this wasn't even a chocolate factory. It was a peanut farm.

ABOVE *A happy group portrait. Note the difference in coloration between the silver fish on the right and the red one on the left. The latter has been in the river longer and is closer to spawning.*

ABOVE *Freshly grilled silver salmon with garlic butter and lemon is hard to beat.*

That evening after supper there were no dentists to be seen, for a seminar was in progress. In businesslike style they had chosen the Karluk River for a convention. Left in the clubroom, among a few others, was a gentle-featured man of sixty-five, Bob Miley from Red Bluff, California, a retired telephone company repairman, who said he had saved for two years for this trip. Now he was hunched over a vise in a corner, under a reading lamp, tying flies, notwithstanding the fact that he'd brought two hundred or so with him.

It was a mild emollient to one's self-esteem to discover that Miley, almost fifty years a fly-fisherman, had also found the Karluk no chocolate factory, at least on the first day. "What are we doing wrong?" I asked him.

Miley gave his answer some thought. "Don't believe it's the pattern," he said. "Just tying these 'cause I like tying flies." He thought again. "We've got to go deeper," he said. "Those fish we're casting to, the ones leaping and slashing on top?

They're not the hitters. Hitting fish are underneath. Those men got 'em on heavy spoons, right? We got to get our flies scratching the bottom. Reckon that's the way they want it."

What I'd been doing, what we'd been doing, was fishing conventionally downstream, forgetting that the cohos and the mighty chinook salmon of the Pacific were a different kettle of fish from Atlantics. At this moment I couldn't help feeling nostalgia for the fish of that other ocean, the ones the Romans, in admiration, had named *salar*, the leaper. "Trouble is," I said, suddenly, petulantly and illogically, "these damn silvers have no history."

Robin Sikes overheard me and said, "Come with me a minute."

This August evening there was light to spare. We walked away from the lodge to a steep earth bank. He took out a knife and started to probe at its side. Soon he had worked free a small, smooth oval stone, flat with a broad groove at each end. He handed it to me.

RIGHT *The view from the Bristol Bay Lodge dock on a quiet morning epitomizes the Alaskan great outdoors.*

"Fishing equipment," Sikes said. "A sinker – six thousand years old maybe." He pointed at the cutaway bank. "See the layers?" he asked. "That's a kitchen midden. We had five anthropologists up here this summer from Bryn Mawr. They found slate knives, axheads and sinkers. They reckoned the early people, the Koniags, moved in here right after the first glaciers had gone through, found the big fish run and stayed." Sikes took some string from his pocket and stretched it round the stone. A sinker, self-evidently. "No history?" he asked. "Man, this has been one of the hottest fishing areas in the entire world for hundreds of years now."

Thousands, more precisely. Sikes warmed to his lecture. The native people had had it to themselves, he said, for most of those six thousand years, until the Russians came in the eighteenth century, pushing the Empire forged by Peter the Great to its ultimate eastern frontier. In particular, it was Alexander Baranvo who first swashbuckled on to Kodiak Island and the Karluk, seeking fur-bearing sea otters. What he found was perhaps the mightiest salmon run in the world – chinooks, sockeyes, humpbacks (pink salmon), dogs (chum salmon) and cohos – which lasted from May until September. "There must have been twenty million fish moving into the river," said Sikes. "And there were no laws."

Massacring many of the Koniags as a prologue, the Russians salted salmon in barrels, then shipped them west. Later they were joined by freebooting Americans, and then came two events that almost destroyed the most prolific salmon resource on earth. The canning process was invented in the 1790s and in 1867 the US purchased Alaska.

When that purchase became known, men fought with crowbars.

ALASKA: FACTFILE

BACKGROUND

Of all the destinations featured in this book, Alaska offers the most diverse range of quarry to the fly-fisherman. As well as five species of Pacific salmon, there are giant rainbow trout, Arctic grayling, Dolly Varden, Arctic char, lake trout and northern pike. Alaska's inaccessibility makes it a haven for these fish and almost nowhere else in the world are fly-fishermen offered such pristine wilderness conditions in which to fish. While all the fish species in Alaska have their devotees, the different types of Pacific salmon generate the most interest. Visiting fishermen from all over the world flock to the forty-ninth State from June to September to sample some of the world's most prolific salmon runs.

King, or chinook, salmon are the largest Pacific salmon and perhaps the most demanding. On most rivers they average a little over 20 lb; 30 lb is nothing to write home about; and 40–50 lb fish are not uncommon. Kings over twice this size have been taken in nets, although a much more modest fish will test your tackle to the full, especially if it is fresh run. Sockeyes, which can be difficult to tempt to the fly, are probably the hardest-fighting Pacific salmon pound for pound; while the silver salmon, with its looks and its propensity for dramatic jumping fights, most closely resembles the Atlantic salmon. Humpback and chum are the least fished-for of all the Pacific species: they are the smallest and lose condition quicker than some of their larger relatives. The sparkling silver of their flanks quickly fades and in its place spawning livery appears, almost as soon as the fish enter fresh water.

WHEN TO GO

Spring in Alaska is the time of snow melt and heavy runoff for most of the river systems. As soon as the flows start to stabilize and the water temperatures to rise, the first runs of king salmon start to enter the river; in a normal year they'll arrive around the second week of June and continue to run until around the end of July. In early July the first runs of

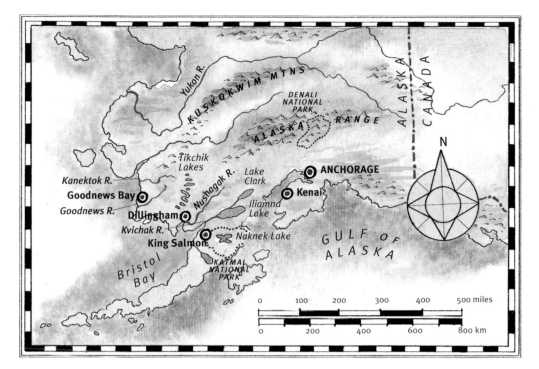

sockeye will be forging upstream, soon to start taking on the dramatic red-and-green spawning dress for which they are so well known. August sees the beginning of the run that so many fishermen await: the dynamic silvers start to enter most watersheds by the second week of August, and may well continue to run right into September.

TACKLE

RODS: For king salmon – single-handed 9 ft for 9–10 wt lines. For sockeyes and silvers – single-handed 9 ft for 6–8 wt lines.

REELS: Large arbor direct-drive with capacity for 150 yards backing.

FLIES 1 *Orange Krystaliser* 2 *Black Matuka* 3 *Babine Special* 4 *Orange Super Comet* 5 *Black Krystaliser* 6 *Green Boss* 7 *Sculpin* 8 *Olive Sculpin* 9 *Eggsucking Leech* 10 *Olive Matuka*

LINES: Fast sinking lines for kings in heavy early water. Sink-tips and floaters for sockeyes and silvers.

LEADERS: 10–15 lb for kings; 8–10 lb for sockeyes and silvers.

FLIES: Matukas, Wooly Buggers, Zonkers, Gray Ghosts, Mickey Finns and Orange-and-White or Red-and-White Bucktails.

Raspberries in the Rain

Norway

ERNEST SCHWIEBERT

"The Laerdal drops through the meadows at Gammleboll, and sweeps past the huge granite walls that buttress the Fagernes highway. Its currents churn against these mossy battlements and dance into the depths of the Wallholen. Salmon hold in its first sixty meters of current. They lie under swirling currents of sapphire and spume, where the stream wells up silken and smooth, before the river grows shallow over a tail of fine cobble. There are often sea trout in those quiet margins, particularly in the weeks to come, but we were after bigger game."

"Oh good Sir, this is a war you sometimes win, and must sometimes expect to lose."

Izaak Walton, 1653

It rained softly through the night.

The mountains were completely shrouded in clouds just after daylight, and the street was wet when I crossed the gardens of the Hotel Lindstrom to breakfast. Great flocks of gulls were wheeling over the tidal reaches of the Laerdal.

The breakfast room was empty, but its cold table was laid and waiting, and the serving girls peered from the kitchen and giggled when I arrived. Breakfast was soft-boiled eggs and goat cheese and brislings in dill sauce, with sweet butter and black pumpernickel, and when I finished my coffee and a small dish of fresh straw-berries, I returned to my room to dress for the river. It was chilly, and the Bergen radio promised cloudy weather and rain. There was an extra pullover in my duffle, and I rummaged for a rain jacket and scarf, since it was cool enough to see one's breath. The fresh hairwing Ackroyds and Orange Charms I had dressed before breakfast were lying on the tiny night table.

The morning ferry from Kaupanger arrived while I was loading the old Mercedes, and its ship's horn resounded through the lower valley, echoing from the steepwalled escarpments.

"Looks like a good morning," Andreas Olsen waved as I reached his cottage, and the famous old gillie clambered into the car.

"The fish like the rain?"

"It seems they do," he nodded thoughtfully, "and the river usually goes down when it rains."

"Goes down when it's raining?"

The veteran gillie smiled indulgently. "Cloudy weather stops the icefields from melting in the mountains," he explained, "and the river seems to fish better with less snow melt."

"Makes sense," I nodded. "Where are we fishing?"

"Kvelde," he said.

Andreas Olsen understood the Laerdal like no other gillie in the valley, since both his father and another legendary riverkeeper, Jens Klingenberg, were dead. Ole Olsen had been the keeper for Lord Henry Portman, and Klingenberg had served two other famous British experts, T.T. Phelps and J.C. Mottram. Andreas Olsen had dressed flies and gillied for the late Prince Axel of Denmark, and his

ABOVE *Anglers must follow the big salmon of the Alta River in a boat, but as the fish begin to tire the canoes are beached and the remainder of the fight is from the shore.*

FLY, OPPOSITE TOP *A Willie Gunn.*

famous son, Olav Olsen, now dressed flies for Prince Harald of Norway.

The road winds south from Laerdalsoyri, past its tiny clapboard houses, and the old churchyard in a dense copse of pines, until there were scattered farmsteads above the town. The windshield wipers were dancing rhythmically as we passed the hayfields and casting platforms at Hunderi. The fields were empty and wet, and no one was building hay fences. Farmers in bright yellow slickers were loading milk cans at the Tonjum crossroads, and there were dairy cattle in the river bottoms. We left the car at the new bridge near the Kvelde Pool.

"Andreas, what did we draw this morning?" I asked.

"Wallholen," he said.

Thomas Falck was already fishing just above the bridge. He waved and shook his head to tell us there was no luck, and we clambered over the stiles and stone fences to reach the footpath along the river. The Wallholen lay several hundred meters far-ther upstream, and it was the pool we had drawn at Rikheim.

The footpath winds past fields of potatoes and cauliflowers and cabbages, and there were thickets of red raspberries at the stile crossings. The wet berries glistened with raindrops and were quite good. We continued along the river, in a corridor of silver birches, with the river tumbling just beyond the trees.

The Laerdal drops through the meadows at Gammleboll, and sweeps past the huge granite walls that buttress the Fagernes highway. Its currents churn against these mossy battlements and dance into the depths of the Wallholen.

Salmon hold in its first sixty meters of current. They lie under swirling currents of sapphire and spume, where the stream wells up silken and smooth, before the river grows shallow over a tail of fine cobble. There are often sea trout in those quiet margins, particularly in the weeks to come, but we were after bigger game.

Olsen was skeptical about my light rod, although he had seen me take a twenty-pound fish with it at Tonjum, with a brace of two-salt fish weighing thirteen.

"But we're fishing small flies," I protested.

"Pray for grilse," he sighed.

Olsen selected one of the traditional Jock Scotts from my Wheatley box, and cautiously knotted it to my tippet. The old gillie led me carefully up the rocky shingle toward the throat of the pool, and stopped to study the river, estimating its character at this height of water.

"Start here," he said.

"They're holding this high in the current?" I asked. "It still seems like pretty heavy water."

"They're holding under the current," he replied.

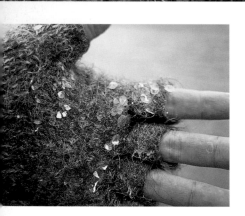

BELOW, TOP AND BOTTOM *Detail of the wrist and tail of a fresh-run Norwegian salmon, and the gloved hand that held it.*

RIGHT *Ted Dalenson, fishing from a traditional Alta River canoe, plays what he thinks is likely the largest salmon he ever hooked; 45 minutes into the battle the fly pulled free. He feels that this fish was over 50 lb. The beautiful light only intensified the drama.*

The false casts switched out, lengthening until they worked back and forth in the drizzling rain, and I dropped the fly well across the current tongue near the masonry abutments. I mended and lowered the rod to start the fly swimming, mended again and again, to slow it through the fast water in the belly of the swing, and began to work it with a teasing rhythm as it emerged from the tumbling spume. I took a step and cast again. Each cast sliced out through the rain, dropping well across the river, and came back enticingly through its concentric swing. Nothing. The heady anticipation of fishing an unfamiliar pool had begun to ebb, once I had fished halfway through its holding water.

"The river seems dead."

"Patience," the old gillie smiled. "There's still another twenty meters of good water to come."

Suddenly the current rhythms changed, seeming to bulge and swell imperceptibly, before two immense swirls came boiling up behind the fly. Olsen was refilling his battered pipe, cupping the bowl between his hands, to shelter it from the mist. "Cast again," he said.

I carefully repeated the cast, attempting to drop the fly in the same place, and mending again, to mute its speed into the belly of the swing. The salmon appeared again like a dark, pewtery apparition, boiling up behind the swimming fly, and the rod doubled over as it turned back with the Jock Scott in its jaws. It held quietly for a few moments, with a few sullen shakes of its great head, and suddenly bolted forty meters downstream, where it cartwheeled into the rain. There was a noisy screech of tires, as a passing motorist stopped to watch.

"How big?"

"Bigger than a grilse," the old man laughed.

Olsen believed it was better than thirty-five pounds. Other cars on the highway were stopping now, and the daily bus to Fagernes stopped too. People were gathering along the granite parapets of the highway, in a phalanx of black umbrellas, shouting encouragement and advice. The big fish jumped again, writhing into the rain like an acrobat, and the crowd gasped. The salmon bored deep into the belly of the pool, shaking its great hookbill viciously among the cobblestones and boulders, and it bolted again. It wallowed in the surface, threshing and throwing water, forcing me to surrender more and more line.

ABOVE *Red barns and birch trees punctuate the Norwegian countryside.*

RIGHT *An expectant angler fishes carefully down a pool on an early-season Laerdal River swollen with snow melt, outside the village of Laerdalsoyri.*

ABOVE *A pastoral view of the beautiful Namsen River valley. The Namsen has a reputation as a big-fish river.*

It was running now, as we scrambled along the rocky shoal, but it stopped again where the currents gathered in the tail shallows. The water bulged over its bulk, where it held like a big stone in the shallows. I prayed and waited. The great fish finally worked slowly back toward deep water, pulling stubbornly against the bellying slack, and returned slowly toward the throat of the pool. There was another clumsy jump that ended in an awkward splash, and the fish surfaced weakly at midstream.

"Getting tired!" I yelled.

The great fish seemed almost finished. Its huge tail fanned and fluttered now, and we worked cautiously upstream, furtively recovering precious lengths of line. I forced the salmon from the heaviest current tongues, until it rolled almost help-lessly against the pressure.

"Get ready!" I muttered prayerfully.

Olsen crouched and waited with the gaff, less visible to the struggling cockfish.

116

ABOVE *Thorpe McKenzie proudly displays the extraordinary 35-lb salmon he caught on the Alta River during a midsummer trip.*

The salmon rolled on its side, working its shiny gillplates with obvious fatigue, and I lowered the rod laterally to force it closer to the waiting gillie. Its great kype and immense shoulders and silvery flanks were visible in the pewtery light.

The veteran riverkeeper was reaching with the gaff, getting ready to strike, and the salmon lazily rolled over. The nylon raked across its pectorals and skull. It was almost within reach when the small Jock Scott came free. The great fish drifted just beyond the gaff, gathered itself in the shallows, and disappeared. The crowd of spectators gasped, and the flock of umbrellas returned to the bus.

"Damn!" I had been waiting to exhale.

The gillie came ashore wordlessly, collected our gear from the bench, and started back down the footpath through the birches. We were in poor spirits, crossing the stiles and fieldstone walls, and stopping to eat raspberries in the rain.

Sometimes a gillie's best skill is his silence.

BELOW *A Temple Dog.*

LEFT *A visiting American angler and his two Norwegian gillies proudly display an evening's catch.*

NORWAY: FACTFILE

BACKGROUND

Fly-fishing for the large Atlantic salmon that run Norwegian rivers was first introduced by the English in the early 1880s. Norway has long been able to boast the highest average size of Atlantic salmon on many of its rivers, and it was for these leviathans of the salmonoid world that the early explorers came. Many stories tell of huge fish caught or vast catches taken. What is extraordinary about Norway is that on the country's premier rivers these stories are still re-enacted. Rivers such as Alta, Namsen and Gaula, and others like them, still produce fish of 40 or even 50 lb every year.

It has not been a continual fishing idyll though. Norway was one of the first nations to close its estuarine nets, and its fish have been plagued by disease which has led to rivers such as the Driva and the Laerdal being closed for rod and line fishing until such time as salmon stocks have recovered.

However, it is still true that Norway must offer the best chance worldwide that fishermen have of hooking and landing the Atlantic salmon of their dreams. Fishing in the land of the midnight sun against a backdrop of stunning fjords, mountains and valleys while soaking up the tradition and history of the place is a special memory for those fishermen lucky enough to have been there.

WHEN TO GO

Above the 60th Parallel in summer, Norwegian nights are short, with perhaps only an hour or two of semi-dark conditions during most of June and July. Throughout Norway on May 31 fishermen feverishly tackle-up their rods in preparation for 12 o'clock midnight and the beginning of another season. It is generally reckoned that the largest fish will come in the first month of the season, with the smaller salmon and grilse run making up the majority of the fishing as the season advances. June and early July will also be the months in which the highest volume of water is in the rivers owing to snow melt from their mountainous catchment areas. On the larger rivers this heavier early water usually dictates a higher proportion of boat fishing. The season ends in August.

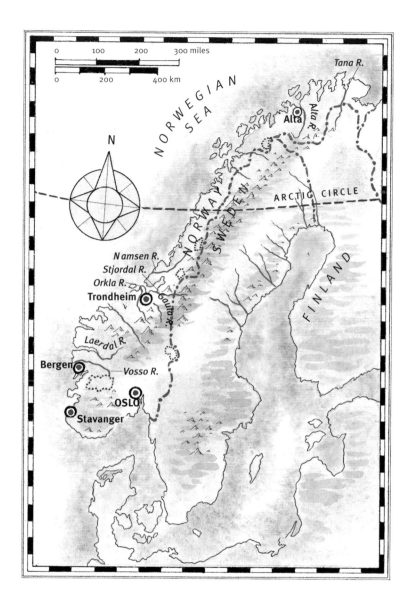

FLIES 1 *Temple Dog*
2 *Baldrick Tube*
3 *Willie Gunn*
4 *Munroe Killer*
5 *Sunray Shadow*
6 *Silver Stoat*

TACKLE

RODS: Double-handed rods, from 13 to 16 ft for 9–11 wt lines.

REELS: Large direct-drive adjustable disk-brake reels to hold fly line and at least 150 yards of 30 lb backing.
LINES: Fast sinking lines for early season fishing, through to intermediates and floaters by the end of the season.

LEADERS: 5–25 lb breaking strain leaders.

FLIES: Large hook sizes are the favourites for traditional hair- and feather-wing patterns such as Green Highlander, Akroyd, General Practitioner and Comally. Tubes and Waddingtons might include Baldricks, Sunray Shadows, Temple Dogs and Willie Gunns.

On Wesley's River

Canada

Tom McGuane

"I arose from bed in the wonderful music of the birds in the forest surrounding the camp. To western ears, the sliding notes of the redstart made a summery mystery. I thought of the warm haze in the skies, the nearness of the sea, the plain thrill of fishing for strong North Atlantic ocean fish whose legend required their seasonal presence in what otherwise was a woodland trout stream. The mind of an angler is stretched to account for this."

Recently, and among people we didn't know that well, my eleven-year-old daughter said something that made jaws drop. She had heard the phrase "the F-word," possibly from a potty-mouthed sibling, and assuming in our house that it must mean fishing, said to a group of guests, "*All my dad cares about is the F-word.*" In the astonished silence that followed this showstopper, she added, "When he's not doing it, he's reading about it."

Well, it's true; but I don't like every kind of it and some of the latest forms of trout fishing as applied in my home state of Montana make me loath to bump into any of its practitioners for fear I will again see the tall man on the banks of Poindexter Slough who was tinting his neutral-colored flies with Magic Markers to match the mayflies rising around him. There's always some little rivulet no one else wants, a brushy bend, a pond back from the road under wild apple trees. Go there.

ABOVE *A Purple Bomber.*

I had an opportunity this summer to escape the latest techout fly-fishing with its whirring splitshot, 7X leaders and transitional subaqueous life-forms imitated in experimental carpet fibers. I spent a week in a portageur canoe ("Not a Bonaventure and not a Gaspé") with Wesley Harrison, who was guiding for his fifty-third year on the Grand Cascapedia River of Quebec. A portageur canoe, which is what Wesley called it, is a broad-bottomed and commodious rivercraft big enough to carry nets and rain gear, that can be driven by a light outboard, and can slip along quietly in the river from drop to drop, as the precise settings of the killock or anchor are called. A bowman is called for to handle the anchor, in this case

a cheerful young Canadian named Jeff, who deferentially helped Wesley move the boat through its daylong ballet on the rapids and meanders of the great river.

I was warned that if I did not fish seriously the entire time that I was on the river, if I repeatedly misstruck fish or failed to turn over my leader in the wind, Wesley would return to shore and put me off the boat. He has taken more than one sport in early with the recommendation that he go elsewhere to learn to fish before coming back. I was tuned up by such admonitions forty years ago on the Pere Marquette River by my father and my "uncle" Ben Ruhl; and there was a certain solace in having the majesty of a great river presumed as a place of seriousness, if not solemnity. These men grew up before the advent of Jet Skis and other entertainment doodads of this suckhole age. The river was your great wife and the very hem of her skirt must be honored.

I arose from bed in the wonderful music of the birds in the forest surrounding the camp. To western ears, the sliding notes of the redstart made a summery mystery. I thought of the warm haze in the skies, the nearness of the sea, the plain thrill of fishing for strong North Atlantic ocean fish whose legend required their seasonal presence in what otherwise was a woodland trout stream. The mind of an angler is stretched to account for this.

I had breakfast with my hosts who aren't particularly anxious for you to know who they are: homemade pastries, homemade jams, tawny local bacon and farm eggs. I gathered my rod and sweater, a book of low-water salmon flies on Patridge Wilson-style hooks, some hard candy to suck at tense moments; then walked across fields of wild strawberries swept by a warm, balsamic breeze. My only fears were

ABOVE *A father and son hook up on the Grand Cascapedia, one of the premier salmon rivers of Quebec, while the local Native American guides steady the boat and prepare to net the fish.*

that I would be struck by lightning or that news of a world war would come over the little radio in the kitchen or that Wesley would kick me out of the canoe.

I met Wesley Harrison and his bowman Jeff. Wesley was a tall, strongly made and cheerful man in his seventies, flannel sleeves rolled over arms that had poled his canoe thousands of miles. Jeff was that rare, quick-witted youngster, without a phony bone in his body. He kept one eye on Wesley to be sure of the right syncopation of effort.

The river was a little dark and I mentioned this to Wesley. He shook his head

ABOVE *The fish of a thousand casts: that's what they call Atlantic salmon when it seems nothing is moving. But just as your thoughts start to wander – bingo! There he is!*

faintly. "Not good," he said. "The old Indian calls this p'ison water." We pushed off and started the motor. I sat in the middle of the canoe and rested my fingertips on my fly rod, laid across the thwarts. I kept one eye on the unscrolling river behind and one on Wesley whose billed cap shifted left and right as he sized up our course.

We passed another canoe on the way with two Mic Mac Indians guiding a well-dressed sport who failed to acknowledge our passing. "Oh, that old Indian feller

there now," said Wesley, "he's quite comical. I asked him yesterday if they were catching anything and he called out, 'Nothing! Fisherman no good!' – He's a comical one that one."

Wesley shut the engine off and tilted it on the narrow transom. Then he grasped the paddle, and, finning it skillfully alongside the ribbed hull, eased us silently downstream to the head of a long pool. "Let 'er go, Jeff," and our bowman dropped the iron. The canoe settled into a stop and the Grand Cascapedia whispered past the hull. "No shipwrecks with a lad like Jeff," said Wesley. He thought for a moment. "If we drowned, poor old Jeff's girlfriend would be running up and down the riverbank crying her heart out." I looked back at Jeff who was gazing at the sky. I got the feeling this had been going on for a while. Then to me, "We'll fish this one to the right."

I thought of my host's father a previous evening, sitting deep in a chair on the screen porch above the river, reciting Izaak Walton, "When the sun is bright and the moon is right, the fish will bite. Maybe." And the great proverb of my Celtic forebears, "It's better to be lucky than to rise early." All sorts of things run through your mind when you look at new water, especially great new water with its concealments and prospects. This really was a fine pool, cut out of stone and the roots of old trees, with a long, deep, trembling run down its center. The water was tea-dark from alder stain but it was clearing rapidly.

I cast my fly, a Green Highlander, in widening arcs, extending one arm's length of line each cast until I had reached my longest cast, all under Wesley's hawklike

gaze. I reeled up, thus signaling Wesley to resume his crouch at the gunwale with his paddle, Jeff to lift the killock, as we moved to the next drop. The current was different here and Wesley kept his paddle in the water to control the yaw of the canoe.

We resumed conversation. I had seen a small valley that stood at an angle to the river and asked Wesley about it. "Oh, a tough life there," said Wesley, "more mealtimes than meals." I murmured, I thought, compassionately; but did catch a glint in Wesley's eye. "There's an old feller up there so poor he has to take his dog down to the gate in a wheelbarrow to bark at strangers." Wesley told me about a Frenchman who lived nearby while I burned a hole in the river looking for a moving shape under my fly. The Frenchman was a high-spirited man whose wife had twins. When Wesley inquired after the babies, the Frenchman (Wesley did the accent) said, "Oh, they're cute little things but they're an awful bother."

I fished this drop very slowly, thinking we were in the heart of the matter. Every so often, a seagull flew overhead reminding me of the ocean not so far away but somehow unimaginable in this beautiful sweetwater stream. At the bottom of the pool, the river went through a cleft in the rock and I thought that must be the end of it. Wesley stared at the pool as my line moved on top of the current. "What's the matter, Mr Salmon, a hot day like this. We'll put you in the cooler and save you the trouble of swimming all the way up stream."

We discussed life in Cascapedia, a small place which like all places, had most of the world's problems, even drugs. "Fine young fellers," said Wesley, "good fellers get on these drugs. Couple of months they look like they crawled through a knot hole." And of course nature: "The Old Indian says the hummingbird goes south by getting into the feathers of the wild goose." He looked at me and shrugged, maybe, maybe not. Then he apologized in case the bowman seemed a bit sleepy: late night with the girlfriend.

Just then, an astonishing thick shape sucked a section of water down around my fly and I hooked a salmon. My reel screeched at the first run and then with wonderful power, the fish was vaulting high over the surface of the pool. I got my fingers inside the arbor of my reel to slow things down but it was clear the fish was not going to be entirely under control for a while. Another jump, this one sideways in a real rip. Somehow, the killock was weighed and Wesley was slipping us over to the gravel bar opposite the pool. I got out to fight the fish while Wesley readied the net and Jeff slid the canoe ashore. Then the fish jumped again and broke the leader.

RIGHT *The wide expanses of forested mountains and river all but dwarf a Matapedia canoe anchored in midstream while anglers cast over a favorite lie.*

Wesley walked over to me, looked at my straight rod. It was silent. Then he asked, quite coolly I thought, "What happened?"

Now he wanted to look over my tackle. The leader, a finely tapered thing, he actively disliked. I buried my own views of leaders and took one of his, tied on another fly, and began fishing the next drop below the one where the salmon, a big salmon, had taken the fly. I knew how it was. The next take could be a week away. There was a cavernous silence in the canoe. I resumed my methodical fishing of the drop, cast, lengthen, cast, lengthen. The waterspeed was picking up lower in the pool and required more careful mending of the line. I kept seeing the fish in the air, hearing the erratic screech of the reel, feeling that slump as the dead rod straightened. And Wesley's question, "What happened?" I wasn't happy.

BELOW *A golden sunset over the Miramichi finds an angler fishing the riffles for running fish moving upstream.*

BELOW *A Green Machine.*

But then I hooked another fish, a hard-running ocean-bright fish; and this one, after several wonderful leaps, ended up in Wesley's net, a big deep hanging silver arc. With a wide smile that confirmed my absolution, Wesley said, "A fresh one, right from the garden!"

We bounced along the river toward the camp, tall ferns thrust through the gunwales to announce our fish. When we landed, Wesley shook my hand and said he'd see me in the morning. "You can't leave us now," he told me. "We're well acquainted from fighting the salmon together!"

I headed back up through the banks of wild strawberries considering a nap, the river poems of Michael Drayton, considering the notion that no one owed me anything.

BELOW *What fly to use for the last pool before supper?*

LEFT *A big, wonderful hen-fish of 24 lb is released back into the clear, clean waters of the Bonaventure.*

CANADA: FACTFILE

BACKGROUND

From Nova Scotia through New Brunswick, Quebec, Labrador and Newfoundland, the Maritime Provinces of Canada can boast more than 400 salmon rivers. These are some of the world's prettiest Atlantic salmon waters and the fish that run them are noted as acrobatic and resilient fighters. A number of the more remote catchments were not fished by fishermen until well into this century, when the advent of floatplanes made them more accessible. Many of the pioneering expeditions were the work of the legendary fly-fisherman Lee Wulff, who was also responsible for revolutionizing several techniques and practices associated with Atlantic salmon fishing, including the "portland" or "riffled hitch" (a method of fishing a conventional wet fly so that it skates across the surface of the water).

The catchments of the Maritime Provinces may not produce the vast numbers of fish that they used to, but many of their names are synonymous with large fish. Rivers such as the Grand Cascapedia, Moisie, Restigouche and Matapedia still produce fish in the 30–40 lb class. Canada is also tireless in trying to improve the runs of salmon to its waters. In May 1998 the Atlantic Salmon Federation's Quebec Council announced a buy-out of the province's remaining commercial nets, and many now feel that the Federation is very close to a buy-out of the last commercial Canadian netting operation. With a long history of strong catch restraints being placed on rod and line fishermen, which has proven effective in improving the number of returning fish, a buy-out of these remaining nets would further enhance all of the province's river catches.

For fly-fishermen thinking of going to these fantastic rivers, the future looks increasingly bright.

WHEN TO GO

As with most Atlantic Salmon destinations, early season fishing can suffer from high water levels and cold temperatures. But by mid-June most Canadian rivers are receiving the first runs of larger mature fish. In mid-July the bulk of the grilse run will have started. While low water and bright sunny conditions can make fish despondent in August, fishing

FLIES *A selection of Bombers – by no means the only flies used in Canadian salmon fishing, but perhaps the most exciting because the salmon's take is visible.*

normally picks up again in September, when the last runs of fresh fish enter the rivers. On some of the region's systems, these late-returning fish can be some of the largest of the year.

TACKLE

RODS: Single-handed 9 ft rod for 7–9 wt line. Double-handed 12–14 ft rods for 8–10 wt lines.
REELS: Direct-drive large arbor reels with capacity for 150 yards of backing plus fly line.

LINES: Mostly floating, though intermediate and sink-tip may be useful in the early season.

LEADERS: At least 8 lb test line; perhaps up to 15 lb.

FLIES: Dry flies – Bombers, Wulffs, Muddlers, Brown Bi-visible and Macintosh. Wet flies – Rusty Rat, Silver Rat, Cosseboom, Blue Charm, Jock Scott, Thunder and Lightning and Black Dose.

Never on Sundays

Scotland

DAVID PROFUMO

"Running a fly down Rocky Cast one evening, there was a flash of grey flank and my small Stoat just below the surface was cancelled like a typing error. The Hardy Perfect made its corncrake rasp as the fish led us down to Fir Dam, where the universe opened along one of its seams and threw out a huge salmon into the air; the sun had gone as we arrived at the place called Paradise, then Mr Murray removed the champagne cork from his gaff-point and leaned over, there was a great convulsion in the margins, and he'd cleeked my prize."

ABOVE *An upstream view of the stunning Glencalvie beat of the River Carron in the Scottish Highlands.*

It didn't start with a salmon, it started with an eel – and I can recall it distinctly because it was the same year we almost burned the castle to the ground, and a French governess pushed my face into some scalding porridge. I was five, and my family had rented this place on Royal Deeside for the holidays. The night of the fire may have gone down in local history but for me the highlight of that summer was the day I first held a rod in my hands. It was a Japanese thing with a red plastic handle, and I lowered a lobworm into a little burn that was spating like gravy: the bootlace eel I hoiked out was my first fish, proudly displayed in the basin of the castle washroom until some adult demanded its removal.

Since then, although I am English, I have spent a happy proportion of my life up North and now I have a home just a raven's flight over the hills from the Dee. I have been lucky enough to fish for salmon in over thirty different Scottish rivers and loch

ABOVE *An afternoon break at the fishing hut on Fir Park pool on the River Dee.*

systems, and I have become an *aficionado*, an amateur, a lover of the sport (what I am not is an expert – a man who knows eighty-seven ways of making love, but can't find himself a girl). These days perhaps I feel a bit unfaithful when I conjure up salmon from an Icelandic foss, or even some chum bar in Alaska, but I always return to Scotland because this is where so much I associate with the culture of angling originally evolved – the floating line, the Spey throw, those malts – and whilst I admit her salmon are getting a bit thin on the ground I believe it is anyway the minor triumphs rather than the huge days that actually make fishing worthwhile.

To many people, fish are unappealing – coldblooded and uncuddly, even in the smaller sizes – but you can see why the salmon is one of the few to share the charisma of some of the terrestrial megafauna such as the elephant or deer. It is a glamorous creature, a nomad struggling up from the dark tides, swapping its silver

BELOW *A Sweep.*

BELOW *Gillie and fisherman discuss strategies on the River Oykel.*

for sackcloth, eventually wasting away in the headwaters of its own birth. Most societies require their fluvial myths, and this is heroic stuff – small wonder that the township of Peebles should derive its motto *Contra nando incrementum* ("There is increase by swimming against") from the spawning run of its local fish. Indeed, there are many parts of Scotland where the harvest of migratory fish once essential for the survival of tribes remains just as crucial to the health of local economies.

You can see this importance ritualized if we go to the very top of the River Tay in mid-January, where the long season opens with a blessing of the fleet. Kenmore, home of Scotland's oldest inn, is a little part of Scotland that the twentieth century forgot to spoil, and each wintry Opening Day there is a sizeable procession of folk marching down to the landing-stage accompanied by skirling pipes. As a sportsman I have a fondness for superstitious sequences designed to make things happen – from the icthyomancy of the Ancient Greeks to the custom of the Wonkgongaru Aborigines that requires their head man to pierce himself somewhere very painful and masculine, ceremonies before the hunt by water were once quite usual; there's no bodypiercing required at Kenmore, just the ladling into the stream of a dram from an ornate *quaich*. Then dozens of anglers can hurry off.

As our piscicidal century creeps to its close, the quest for a Scottish springer has become a bit of a unicorn hunt, but in its heyday the *locus classicus* for these big beauties was Loch Tay itself; I think the record for this hotel was Colonel Murray's thirty-one fresh fish averaging eighteen pounds (you used to pay the gillie three shillings and eightpence a day, plus a modest "allouance" of whisky to fuel him as he trolled you round the loch). These days as you send your wooden Devon strumming over some desirable residence in the river you're more likely to be rewarded with a pull from a spent *kelt*, or *baggart* (a salmon that has not shed her ova, sometimes known as a *thwarted matron*), but although these must naturally be returned unscathed they still give a thrill in the chill as they offer that first pulsing resistance against the current. I'm not one of those purists who'd rather stick his arm in an industrial log-chipper than use anything except a fly, but I do like to wave my rod about and I find the *harling* that goes on here a little dull. Mind you, this is Scotland's largest river and it can be a job to cover, especially in the lower reaches below Macbeth country, where its pools rejoice in names such as Fire Shot, Kill Moo and Rumbling Stane.

The Tay also has a history of huge fish unrivalled in Britain (the Wye in the 1930s might just have pipped it to the post), and it was here of course that our record salmon was landed by Miss Georgina Ballantine, a gillie's daughter, on October 7 1922; she killed it in the Boat Pool on Glendelvine Water after a struggle lasting two hours. She liked to recount how it was displayed in the window of Malloch's tackle shop in Perth and she overheard a local man say, "Nae woman ever took a fish like this … that's a lee, anyway!" Almost as intriguing is the saga of the fish lost by G.F. Browne, Bishop of Bristol, in 1868 just by the junction with the Earn. After ten hours the gut parted: one account ends, "Jimmy rows home without a word, and neither he nor the fisherman will ever get over it." It is said a fish was later netted downstream with the episcopal minnow in its mouth, and weighed seventy-one pounds.

BELOW *A Crystal Ally's Shrimp.*

BELOW *A wee dram of fine whisky helps ease the pain of not catching a salmon on the Dee.*

I don't get to do much serious fishing in the summer, because we spend our time in the Outer Hebrides with our children, rummaging around in rockpools or pursuing sticklebacks with butterfly nets. But when I was growing up I had two wonderful angling mentors, and the summers meant salmon in Sutherland.

My uncle was a formidable, pipe-smoking sportsman practically stone deaf from flying open-cockpit aircraft in the Great War. He possessed a cartridge bag fashioned from the skin of a rogue lion he had once been obliged to shoot during his gubernatorial days in West Africa, and a hipflask capable of containing almost an entire bottle of whisky (he left both these heirlooms to me). Through his estate near the east coast ran the Fleet, one of those modest, unkempt spate rivers in which the Highlands abound, with a succession of bonsai pools that fished well for a few hours after each flood from July onwards, the grand total for that beat being perhaps a dozen salmon per season. Here at the age of twelve, after two summers of trying, I caught my first salmon – rather a tired grilse – from The Stepping Stones, using a Grant Vibration greenheart rod spliced with leather bindings. In attendance was the second mentor, Mr George Murray, my uncle's personal gillie.

As fishing guides go, the Scottish gillie is famously a race apart: some are genuinely water wizards, others are no better than reluctant caddies eager to guzzle your Scotch. Mr Murray – as I always called him – was a companion from Central Casting. His poker face, long considered the badge of a true Highland professional, hid both a sunny disposition and a pawky wit. During my teenage years as his sorcerer's apprentice I learned much from him – that you always refer to a salmon as "a fish", that a big fly can sometimes be effective in low water – but most of all he showed by example how one should always enjoy time spent on the water, irrespective of how the sport is going. This sounds obvious, but since then I've seen many anglers forget that the point is to have fun. From my hours spent with that quiet, gentle man I began to understand the paradox of fishing – how to accept both its illusion of treasure trove and the constant spectre of disappointment.

OPPOSITE *A view downstream toward the Rock Pool on the River Oykel.*

Every other day – with the exception of Sundays, because of course no salmon fishing is allowed on the Sabbath – my uncle took a beat on the nearby Shin, a short hydro-controlled river that debouches into the Kyle of Sutherland alongside those other fine waters the Carron, Cassley and Oykel. Like them, it is a challenging river with formidable, bouldery pots and moiling chestnut-brown runs, not least of which is the celebrated Falls Pool itself, one of the most spectacular salmon leaps anywhere I know. To winkle out Shin fish you often had to hold your fly over a churning lie on a long rod (the sinuous Collie Dog lure was especially favoured), sometimes hanging off a rockface with your other hand. The salmon ran big for summer fish, too, and once you hooked one the commando tactics had only just begun. No fly-fishing could have been better designed to intrigue a fanatical teenager, and throughout those lank-locked, resentful years, when adults understood zilch and testosterone mood-swings clouded my vision, there was always the prospect of that river and its succession of roaring gorges.

Running a fly down Rocky Cast one evening, there was a flash of grey flank and my small Stoat just below the surface was cancelled like a typing error. The Hardy Perfect made its corncrake rasp as the fish led us down to Fir Dam, where the universe opened along one of its seams and threw out a huge salmon into the air; the sun had gone as we arrived at the place called Paradise, then Mr Murray removed the champagne cork from his gaff-point and leaned over, there was a great convulsion in the margins, and he'd cleeked my prize. It was a cock fish of twenty-one pounds, beaked like Punchinello. I have never forgotten the sight of him, squirming there on the metal, his great eye seeming to stare at me as he was hoist fatally into the half-light, a low gargling sound escaping from his throat. I was then fifteen years old.

Golden Ages are forever receding, and one can readily discover in the literature of the last century grumbles that the fishing is not what it was (the great fairy-tale collector Andrew Lang was at it, for instance, in his *Angling Sketches*, 1891); but few would deny that Scottish salmon fishing in the modern period is in a state of crisis. In addition to the high-seas netting, these stocks still have to contend with licensed drift-netters off the north-east coast of England, a disproportionate seal population, and now the threat of estuarial mariculture. The concentrations of parasitic lice around the salmon cages that clog the sea lochs of Scotland seem to be capable of damaging migratory fish in as yet unpredictable ways – several outbreaks of Infectious Salmon Anaemia were confirmed in 1998, the first ever in British fish farms.

ABOVE *George Ross, fishery manager on the River Oykel, puts the net under a fresh-run spring salmon.*

Meanwhile, to the amazement of many North American anglers who have been practising it for years, catch and release appears to be something that sharply divides the British game-fishing community, though our millions of coarse anglers have never found much problem with the concept. Old habits certainly die hard, but let's hope the salmon doesn't die out completely first.

Such are the years of tradition behind salmon fishing here that when I am wading in certain Scottish waters I am peculiarly aware of both the quick and the dead. It might be Wood on the Dee, Ashley-Cooper on the Spey, or any number of more anonymous forebears who have stood in a certain spot and watched the water jump up behind the same rock, but I am alive to their historical presence. (Sometimes I vaguely wonder if, a century hence, a similarly minded chap might recall how the present writer used to cast here with his superannuated carbon poles and manual reels, in the days when there were still wild fish, but the prospect of borrowed time is a gloomy one.) This sensation is strongest during my autumn visits to a fabled beat of the Middle Tweed, a river I have been privileged enough to fish during one of its prime weeks for the past twenty-two years. My historical fancy does not need much of a spur, for these are the very pools where William Scrope often cast while working on his *Days and Nights of Salmon Fishing* (1843), one of the few genuine classics on the subject; indeed each year, like the page of King Wenceslas, I tread in his steps, mindful of his warning "never go into the water deeper than the fifth button of your waistcoat", and to cease wading when the legs turn black. Scrope dwelt at Melrose, and was a close friend of the Laird of Abbotsford, Sir Walter Scott, whose novels (such as *Waverley* and *Rob Roy*) had done so much to make Scotland a voguish destination for angler-Saxons, restoring its clannish image tarnished to Southern eyes since the days of Jacobitism.

Autumn is anyway my favourite season here, with the slow fire of its colours burning through the leafscapes of beech and birch and the big stream rattling beneath sandstone cliffs of Tuscan pink. These borderlands look deceptively serene, though, and the land is steeped in the blood of Roman legionaries, reivers, moss-troopers and other feuding bandits; nearby the Scots murdered the last two Picts, to get their recipe for heather ale; in the distance rise the Eildon Hills, split into three by the Devil at the behest of Auld Michael Scot, the wizard who languishes in Dante's *Purgatorio*. Something of all this surely lingers, making the hand shake and the bloodstream tingle as your puny lure sweeps across the dark pools. Unless there is a rare drought – in which case I have to amuse my party with picnics and John Barleycorn – you expect to fish large, slow, deepish flies at this time of year, often Tweed-style from the back of a rowed boat. And so it was that I caught my largest-ever Atlantic here, a fish weighing twenty-eight pounds: a photograph of us hangs in the Rogue's Gallery at the Ednam House Hotel in Kelso, and I was so pleased with this achievement that I once drove a Dutch translator all the way down from Edinburgh, just to see the picture. When the autumn runs are on, the hallway of this famous hotel is sometimes paved with silver bodies awaiting

ABOVE *To reach some very enticing fishing pools in the gorge on the upper Kirkaig River requires a strenuous scramble.*

dispatch to the smokery, for the back-end Tweed salmon when absolutely fresh are amongst the finest of all Scottish fish.

It is in the still charming market town of Kelso that there lies buried another of my angling author-heroes, Thomas Tod Stoddart, who in his time (he died in 1880) was reputed to have fished more Scottish waters than anyone else; his diaries over fifty years suggest the taking of 67,419 fish, of which some 928 were salmon. He qualified at the law, but never found time to practise. In later life he was asked by one of his friends, who had risen to the rank of sheriff, what he was now doing. "Doing? *Doing?*" came the reply. "Mon, I'm an angler."

There is no guaranteed bonanza every autumn, of course, and more likely would be the experience I had not long ago, with John our able boatman. Fish were scarce, the river was thin and the colour of bitter ale, morale was low. He took me down to the Braes pool around teatime, and almost at once we had a tunk on the line, but the take never developed; at such times I always apply SWAG methodology (Scientific Wild-Assed Guess), so we changed the tube, and something must have looked slightly more plausible because a couple of casts later, as that fly came off the spine of the current, I felt a decent draw, the loop of line slipped through my fingers, and I was able to set the iron. The fish thrashed at once on the surface – seldom the sign of a good hook-hold – displaying a chrome fuselage of agreeable proportions, and I began to play him as gingerly as if I'd never before been attached to a salmon. After ten minutes of emotionally elastic time John murmured, "That's about grand now, sir", lifted the iron hoop of his massive landing-net, and there we had him, a cock of eighteen pounds, tideliced, my only catch of the week. "Not bad for a couple of amateurs," grinned John, who has worked on rivers since he was a boy. We walked back up to the cottage for a drink, comrades in arms.

Fishing stories should have a beginning, a middle and an end – though not necessarily in that order. Last year I drove my wife up to Deeside to revisit Braemar Castle, now a museum. Its stone stairwell and Rapunzel towers looked so much smaller than when I was a boy, but inside the door on the right was a souvenir shop that I was pretty sure had been the place. Yes, the lady serving there confirmed, it was originally the washroom, and there was the old marble basin. I knew it must have been nearly forty years since any boy left an eel there.

As an angler I sometimes think I may be on a quest for something that was lost, of which perhaps the fish is only a symbol.

ABOVE *The tea-colored waters of the Kirkaig flow down from the Scottish Highlands to the sea.*

LEFT *A lone angler admires the beauty of the upper Dee valley, as he prepares to cast.*

SCOTLAND: FACTFILE

BACKGROUND

If the English chalkstreams represent the birthplace of modern trout fishing, then Scotland, without question, is the place where most of the accepted techniques of fly-fishing for Atlantic salmon were developed. With an enormous wealth and diversity of rivers, from small highland spate streams such as the Kirkaig or Inver, to mighty systems like the Tay or Tweed, Scotland has long been recognized as one of the world's premier destinations for Atlantic salmon fishing.

Although there have been worrying declines in the numbers of returning fish over the past couple of decades, Scotland remains for many fishermen the quintessential Atlantic salmon-fishing experience. There can be few moments as rewarding in a fisherman's life as toasting success with a friendly gillie over a dram of whisky, while listening to the grouse calling from the heathered hillsides bordering the river.

WHEN TO GO

Precise legal dates vary according to the catchment being fished, but generally speaking the season starts around mid-January and ends in late November. Returning salmon and grilse in Scotland arrive at varying points of the season. Traditionally, the spring fish were the ultimate challenge. These fish are mature salmon, normally of high average size, that run any time between January and June. However, "spring fishing" seems to have been affected most by the recent declines in Scotland, with the result that now it is the summer run of salmon and grilse that makes up the majority of the most reliable fishing. On some of the larger rivers the autumn run of mature salmon is the final highlight of the season and with good volumes of water in the rivers (on which the fish can ascend a system), sport can be prolific until the last days of the season.

On many rivers in Scotland this autumn run of big fish has almost entirely superseded spring fishing, and it is also likely that this period will demand the highest rent and be hardest to gain access to. It is always wise to enquire early on if you wish to buy fishing during this time.

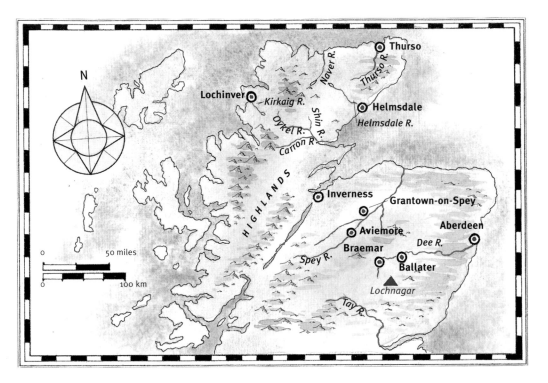

TACKLE

RODS: On smaller rivers, single-handed rods, 9–10½ ft for 7–9 wt lines. On larger rivers, double-handed rods, 12½–15 ft for 9–11 wt lines.

REELS: Large direct-drive reels with or without a drag system.

LINES: A broad selection (depending on water height and temperature), from floating through sink-tips and intermediate to fast sinking.

LEADERS: Lighter leaders, 8–12 lb, during the summer months, but as strong as 15–20 lb for heavier water and bigger fish in spring or autumn.

FLIES: Most rivers have favourites: speak to a local tackle shop or to your gillie. Size of fly is also a factor, dependent on water temperature and height. Keep a fly box stocked with small double- and single-hooked flies for summer, Waddingtons and tubes for spring/autumn. Patterns include Blue Charm, Black Ranger, Ally's Shrimp, Torrish, Dusty Miller, Munroe Killer, Silver Doctor and Green Highlander.

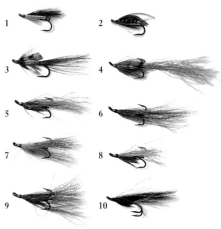

FLIES 1 *Arndilly Fancy* 2 *Sweep* 3 *Stewart Shrimp*
4 *Ally's Shrimp* 5 *Munroe Killer* 6 *Willie Gunn*
7 *Hairy Mary* 8 *Garry Dog* 9 *Silver Stoat*
10 *Crystal Sweep*

OPPOSITE *One evening while walking just below the junction of the Tweed and the Teviot, I spotted an angler with his rod bent double, obviously into a good fish. I ran down to the river bank just in time to capture this splendid picture of the hero and his prize.*

Grimsa Journal

Iceland

Nick Lyons

"Each day you learn a bit more. The salmon react in a new way, striking in the lower end of the pool, in the slick; you learn the slow and steady Crossfield retrieve for water without sufficient current to swing the fly, or how to vibrate your rod horizontally to induce a take. You cast a bit better and you learn the virtue of careful casting by the increased interest the fish show when your flies land three inches rather than ten from the far bank. When the salmon roll or jump you think of dry flies — but they won't work here any more than you'll find a mosquito: bad trade."

SUNDAY NIGHT: Salmon. There are salmon everywhere: salmon leaping the falls behind the lodge, their force astonishing; salmon and salmon rivers – this year's, last year's – in everyone's talk; smoked and poached salmon on the table; on the wall, old and new photographs of men with notable salmon; salmon statistics in the log, with pool, fly, and size listed; salmon in my dreams.

And at dinner, at eleven o'clock, after the first evening of fishing, almost everyone said they had taken a few. Schwiebert took one ten minutes after we got to the river – a bright six-pounder in one of the lower pools. Dick Talleur said he was no longer "a virgin": he had taken his first, lost a second. Joe Rosch, who had never fished for them, brought back two – one better than twelve pounds. He said his hands and knees were shaking after it was netted; he said that, from the excitement, he had fallen flush into the river.

The Grimsa is low but it is filled with salmon. Ten times this afternoon, before we fished, I walked back to the falls, where salmon – some small, some perhaps ten

148

to fifteen pounds – were making their headlong, vital, terrible, exultant leaps at the top of the rush of white water. In the foam and swirl below the falls you could see a tail, a back, flick black out of the white boil. How bright and powerful they are. One four-pounder kept missing the falls and leaping smack into wet lava. I do silly things, too, when caught in the spawning urge.

I have never fished for salmon, but I am catching salmon fever. Perhaps I won't get any. Tonight I was bewildered. I made cast after cast with my #10 rod and double-hooked Blue Charm: across and downstream, then a little half-step and another cast across and downstream. Nothing. Nothing whatsoever. The worst of it was that fish were jumping, coming clear of the water and falling back every few minutes. Big fish. Bigger fish than I had ever seen in a river. Sleek, silver, determined fish. I had not a tick. I went back over my beat four times and moved not one fish.

After a spell, inching downriver along the lava and lava-rubble bottom, watching the crystalline water that appears devoid of all life but for the salmon, you begin

BELOW *Doug Larsen casting a long line in the wading pool of Beat 1 on a morning when the river was full of fish.*

BELOW *A Blue Charm.*

to think you will never catch one of these fish. There seems so little logic to it. Sparse once told me: "By God, the beggar isn't even feeding when he's in the river. If a fish rises to my fly, I want to know why." I have not the slightest notion how to get these mysterious fish to move. Even the flies have strange names: Blue Charm, Black Fairy, Thunder and Lightning, Hairy Mary, Green Butt, Silver Rat. In sizes #6 to #10, double-hooked. Which to use?

Still, what a lot of fun we have had so far. We got to Reykjavik at nine Saturday morning, slept, and walked through the closed town (except for Talleur, who is training for the Montreal marathon and *ran* a short ten miles). The city, built mostly of concrete, since there are few trees, is quaint, even charming. Woolens, silver-work, and ceramics are the chief wares – and they're very handsome. Then we had dinner at Naust, which Ernest said was the finest restaurant in Iceland. The place is like an old sailing ship, with round windows and name-plates of old ships at each table. We ate graflax – which is raw salmon treated with herbs, buried in the earth, then served with mustard and brown-sugar sauce – and then the others chose grilled baby-lobster tails, an Icelandic specialty; I had British beef and we all drank a lot of wine and then had ice cream and brandy. Ernest told us about the early witch hunts in Iceland, which ended when someone said: "Hey, you fellows are killing off the most interesting girls in town." And Dan Callaghan told one about a guy who ate a couple of stone-flies, washed them down with a glass of wine, paused, and said, "The wine's not right." Talleur was there, and Bob Dodge (who's paired with me for the week), and Bob Buckmaster, who has read and loved Plunket-Greene's *Where the Bright Waters*

Meet, and any man who's liked that book I know I am going to like. Anne and Dick Strain, the Perry Joneses, and Joe Rosch, the others in our party, ate elsewhere. We are from Iowa and Albany, New York City and Bellefontaine, North Carolina and Oregon, and we are all in pursuit of this fish bright from the sea, about which I know less than nothing.

The two-hour bus trip from Reykjavik to the Grimsa Lodge this morning wound past the Hvalfjord, which served as an American naval base during the war, and into the Iceland landscape, which is stark, treeless, and curiously beautiful.

Now it is 11.30 and we are settled into the well-appointed lodge that Schwiebert built and there is still light in the sky and I am exhausted. I am also high-keyed, tense. I know this kind of intense fishing. It will be necessary to catch a fish or two before the edge is off. Maybe tomorrow.

MONDAY AFTERNOON: Got my first salmon late this morning on Beat 3, the Strengir. I had fished hard since seven o'clock, casting across and downstream time after time. Buckmaster had given me a crash course on how to tie and fish the riffle hitch. An interesting technique. Since the fly is visible, the take is more dramatic than when the fly is fished conventionally. After a few hours I tried it and an hour later saw a good fish flash. I held back my impulse to strike, then struck and felt him.

The fish went to the bottom of a heavy riffle, shook its head, and sulked for five minutes. I could not budge it. Then it went a bit upstream, then down into the next pool. And in ten more minutes, Gumi, our gillie, netted it. I was thrilled to get a first salmon, a seven-pounder, but, except for the force of the thing, disappointed in the fight. It had not jumped. It had not taken me into the backing. "Brown salmon," said Buckmaster at lunch. "He's been in the river too long. They don't eat, you know, and lose something every day." This not-eating inspired me. I wished I could learn how to not-eat for three months at a stretch. But the food at the lodge – heaping plates of lamb, halibut, salmon, potatoes, and irresistible desserts – is too good.

I got another fish soon after the first, about four pounds, then struck a fish bright from the sea. It went off like a firecracker, leaped, got below me, let me get below it, and finally I beached it. A good morning. The edge is off.

Fished with Buckmaster this afternoon. What a lot of fun he is to be with. Peppery. Wise about salmon. Full of stories. We were on a difficult pool called, with good reason, "Horrible." Bob uses only a fly he ties called the Iowa Squirrel Tail, in fairly large sizes, with a riffle hitch, and he was determined to get one. He cast long and with great skill and then riffled the fly into the slick before a falls. Nothing. Then we went upstream with Topy, his gillie, and the two of them coached me into catching a small sea trout. Bob went back to "Horrible" and worked hard for more than an hour but caught nothing. Still, we'd found a lot to laugh about and the company was awfully good, so the afternoon was a delight. "There's more to fishing than to fish."

"What you're looking for," Schwiebert said, "is a salmon with an itch." I have been looking awfully hard. I don't even know what day it is. My right hand is becoming locked in the casting position, and at night I can feel the thrust of the Grimsa against me and inside me that rhythmic, endless pattern of casting across and downstream, inching forward a half-step, then another cast, then watching the fly rise and sweep across with that pretty little "vee." I've caught nothing in several sessions now, and the wind has become raw, snarling. My casting hand is blotched and swollen from sun and wind and a certain lunatic look has come into my eyes.

Anne and Dick Strain invited me to fish with them this afternoon and I did, on the Strengir again. Anne is avidly looking for new species of birds and is a fount of information about them and about the flora. She pointed out the alpine thyme

BELOW *Mike Fitzgerald casting a long line over the reflecting waters of the Laxá I Adaldal.*

clustered in small patches of bright purple everywhere, cotton-grass, yellow hawk-weed, and pink thrift. I can recognize the whimbrel, with its long curved bill, and the arctic tern.

Dick took two good fish in the last of the five Strengir runs, then, exhausted from casting my heavy rod into the wind, I lent it to him: whereupon he promptly took a third salmon. I tried for another hour but raised not a fish. Then Sven, their gillie, came by and I lent him the rod: whereupon he promptly hooked a good salmon. They called it the Lucky Rod. I have begun to wonder if my first three salmon weren't flukes. Will I ever get another?

Fishing intensely, you grow not to see yourself. Ernest told me at lunch that salmon fishing makes manic-depressives of us all. I feel low. Is it because Bob Dodge got such a fine bright fish this morning, then another, while I got none? I hope not. I enjoyed watching him fight that fish for nearly a half-hour, then net it. It was about nine pounds and terribly strong, and it jumped and ran and when he finally had it his hands were trembling. We took a dozen photographs of him there on Beat 1, holding the fish by the tail, with the falls and the lodge in the background. His excitement was irrepressible. He went up to the lodge, got some scotch, which we all drank riverside, and said, "If I don't get another fish this week, I'll be satisfied."

But this afternoon I feel low, and it is apparently visible, and I still wonder if I'll ever get another salmon.

More snarling wind and cold but no rain. I got one seven-pound fish, the only salmon of the afternoon by anyone in the party. Is it Tuesday?

Every morning we breakfast, a few at a time, as we get up. A buffet of bread, butter, marmalade, sardines in tomato sauce, cereal, and black coffee is laid out, and we can add two eggs cooked to order with ham or bacon. I always sit facing the window, where I can watch the water and the falls. Fewer salmon are leaping now. We need rain.

Then we rouse our partner, head to the wet room, and put on waders and vest. It is cold in the morning and I have been wearing a cotton shirt, a Cambrian Flyfisher's sweater, and an ochre guide's shirt; yesterday I had to add a scarf. Everyone else has felt soles on their waders, which hold well on the lava; I wear my cleated soft-aluminum and felt rubbers, which have proved excellent.

RIGHT *The quiet peacefulness of the lovely Laxá I Adaldal will linger for ever in your memory.*

Our gear is virtually what you would use for large trout: a rod for an 8 line (which I have switched to from my 10), 18-pound test backing (which no one has needed yet), and a heavy leader, 12-pound test and up. The best flies have been the Blue Charm, Rusty Rat, Collie Dog, and Black Tube, all on a double hook, in the smaller sizes.

You learn to fish the lies, not the rise. You begin to *see* the line in your dreams as the week progresses and you rotate beats. Fishing until ten, then talking another few hours, then rising early and spending long hours on your feet, everyone gets tired. Joe has started to skip supper. Some of us have skipped part of a morning's fishing, others rest when their turn at "Horrible" comes. Talleur rested by running sixteen miles yesterday.

In the mornings at seven, and then again at four, the gillies wait outside the wet room. Most of them speak English reasonably well; only Ernest, among us, speaks some Icelandic, which someone told me is not a language but a throat disease.

Each day you learn a bit more. The salmon react in a new way, striking in the lower end of the pool, in the slick; you learn the slow and steady Crossfield retrieve for water without sufficient current to swing the fly, or how to vibrate your rod horizontally to induce a take. You cast a bit better and you learn the virtue of careful casting by the increased interest the fish show when your flies land three inches rather than ten from the far bank. When the salmon roll or jump you think of dry flies – but they won't work here any more than you'll find a mosquito: bad trade. You learn to shorten your leader to seven feet, 16-pound test, against stiff wind, and that this does not bother the fish a whit. When a salmon is on, you have a fish with saltwater size and power in trout-stream conditions, and you remember that Earl West told you to play these fish hard, that a half-minute's rest and you have a fresh salmon on again – so you add more pressure and are amazed that you have not yet lost a fish among the five – or is it six? – you've caught so far.

You watch Schwiebert carefully. He is deft, economical, wise about this river. He teaches you the lies and how much skill truly matters. He knows the history of each pool.

And, knowing the river itself more intimately each day, you look forward with greater expectation to the rotation of the beat. You know the beats better and you have more confidence that you can do this thing. This morning we have Beat 5, which has been fishing extremely well. I think about that as I step out of the wet room and walk with Bob toward Gumi's car.

Joe looked shaken tonight. He had lost a big salmon. Very big. He had seen the fish roll just above the falls of Beat 3 and had tied on a small Blue Charm, cast slightly

LEFT *Nupafossbrun or the Bridge Pool at Beat 7 is a tough place to land a fish – just ask Art Lee.*

BELOW *An angler about to try to hand-tail a salmon in the boat pool at Beat 3 of the Laxá I Adaldal.*

upstream, mended twice, and watched the huge fish take it solidly. The salmon leaped, raced upriver, settled into the pool, then, after ten minutes, leaped again and headed for the falls. Joe decided to try to turn him and the fly pulled free. Now he thinks he should have let the fish go down the falls; he charted the route and thinks he could have followed it. There was much talk and the consensus was that this would have been wisest. The gillie thought the fish would have gone twenty pounds, perhaps more.

Joe was shaken but he has caught an unforgettable memory.

I am fishing his beat tomorrow and asked him to map out the spot. Still no rain.

An interesting afternoon with Bob Dodge. We fished a long flat stretch the others call "The Lake." Perhaps sixty or more salmon are stacked up here, waiting for higher water, and Dan Callaghan and Perry Jones have taken good fish here. Bob went across stream, inched over to the lip of the bluff, and served as "point man" for me. But I could not, though I cast over the salmon many times, move any of them.

Later we went upriver and each took a good fish in broken water. We are beginning to know a bit more about the river and about salmon fishing, and we have at least some confidence that anyone who can use a fly rod reasonably well can take fish. Iceland is not the moon and salmon fishing is not astro-physics.

A flash of bright silver. The fly turning out of the eddy, buffaloing downstream. The tooled lunge. Up, out of the black near the rock he came, into white water, his back curved and turning. Up and out and then down on the fly as it gained speed and began to zip. I waited. And waited. There! I struck, felt the fish throb, and then he careened off, down toward the rapids. Forty, fifty feet of line. Sixty. The first foot of backing came through my fingers.

Then he stopped, shook his head, started off again, and leaped, smashing the water, shaking, and falling back.

Fifteen minutes later I had him on my side of the river. I looked up and saw a dozen cars lined along the bridge, watching. The salmon jumped again, ten feet from me. Ten minutes later he turned to his side and I led him to shallow water. The fish was ten pounds, bright silver, and bolted off when I disengaged the fly.

It is Thursday.

FRIDAY NIGHT: I tailed my first salmon today, a nine-pounder from Beat 5. Dick Talleur was there and got out his camera.

"No!" I called to him, hiding my face. "I've made my reputation by not-catching fish."

"No one deserves a fish like that more than you, Nicky," he said, "after all your family disasters."

"My reputation …"

"I won't blackmail you," he said, clicking off a couple of shots.

When I had gotten a good grip on the salmon's tail, I raised the fish high and kept it high, and kept smiling, long after Dick had stopped shooting.

A little later, upriver, I had four good strikes and could not come up with a fish. Buckmaster kept asking if I was striking too fast. "No," I said, after checking my fly, after discovering that I had busted off both points on the double-hooked fly, "just fishing not wisely but too true to form."

Anne Strain has seen and identified twenty-six different birds, including the gyr-falcon, red-necked phalarope, black-tailed godwit, white wagtail, turnstone, merlin, arctic redpoll, and wheatear. I like the names. I should watch the water a bit less, the sky more. It is strangely beautiful here – spare, the meadows in varying shades of green, spotted, white, and brown Icelandic ponies drinking at the river, the gray streaks of lava everywhere, the snow-splotched mountains, the vast Montana-like space, that little red-roofed Lutheran church on the hillside, the neat farms, sheep everywhere, places where you can look up a valley at four, five waterfalls, one over the other, silver in the sunshine, sunsets the color of salmon flesh, and the light, the light that is always here, even late into the night, making the days longer, fuller.

ABOVE *Full of expectation, an angler walks out to the river on his last evening.*

SUNDAY MORNING: I am exhausted. We leave for the plane in an hour.

Last night Talleur and Buckmaster asked me to go to a local dance with them. Bob wanted to know more about the people. I realized that all I know of Iceland was Snorri Sturluson and *Egil's Saga*, read in graduate school, and that the country had 222,000 people, rampant inflation, gorgeous sweaters, and great salmon rivers. We left at one o'clock at night, in a Land Rover packed with young gillies, the cook, and a couple of pretty girls working at the lodge.

BELOW *A Sweep.*

Images: the jammed dancehall and Bob Buckmaster, who is past sixty-five, doing a convincing hustle or rope or robot or whatever it's called; the blinking lights; rock in Icelandic; the young eager faces; Talleur breaking training with a vengeance; the trip back at five in the morning, as the light broke, drinking bitter Brennivin (known locally, and for good reason, as "the black death"), watching thermal geysers and meandering salmon rivers taking the first glints of light, and all singing, at the top of our lungs, in English, "When the Saints Come Marching In."

Then Bob Dodge and I were out at seven, because we had the most productive beat, and I could hardly stand. But I took a good salmon quickly and that seemed a good way to end matters. "Take up your swords," I rumbled, "the morning dew shall rust them," gave my rod to Gumi, and leaned back in the car to dream of the terrible swift strike of the salmon.

Meanwhile, Bob hit into a slew of salmon with an itch, had ten good strikes, missed a few, hooked and lost a few, and took four fish. A better way to end matters.

Now we're packed and ready to leave. It has been a splendid, memorable week. Too brief. Schwiebert and Callaghan caught the most fish, over twenty each, and Anne Strain got a magnificent nineteen-pounder that struck at ten o'clock and fought her until after eleven last night. I got enough.

There is already talk of coming back. The phrase "trip of a life-time" has been used. There is talk about the effect of this place.

But is Talleur really serious about training on graflax and peanut butter?

BELOW *The rocky ledges of the Grimsa River epitomize the stark, barren, windswept image of Icelandic salmon fishing.*

ICELAND: FACTFILE

BACKGROUND

"The Land of Ice and Fire", as Iceland is sometimes known, is an extraordinary country. In this raw and desolate landscape, it feels very much as though the forces that shaped it are still at work. There are some hundred or so rivers in Iceland that hold salmon, the best of which are located on the north and west coasts, with a handful on the south coast. Almost half of these are classified as first-class rivers, capable of yielding prodigious numbers of fish to rod and line.

While many rivers are privately owned, the Government places its own regulations on the fishing. For example, strict controls govern the number of fishermen allowed to fish each river. So when analysing catch statistics, fishermen should always enquire how many "rod-days" are actually fished in a season.

As the world has noticed diminishing catches of Atlantic salmon, so the Icelanders have become ever more aware of the measures necessary to conserve them. "Catch and release" is no longer an alien phrase in Iceland; the law requires you to disinfect your tackle on entering the country to reduce risk of disease; and the hatchery work here is among the most advanced in the world. The Atlantic salmon-fishing world also owes one Icelander in particular a great debt: Orri Vigfussen has tirelessly campaigned for the removal of open sea and coastal nets throughout the salmon's range, resulting in a new worldwide public awareness of the plight of salmon.

Perhaps the most fascinating aspect of fishing in Iceland is that most of its rivers are crystal clear for much of the season. This offers fly-fishermen unrivalled opportunities actually to gauge the fish's reaction to each successive fly offered. There can be few greater thrills in Atlantic salmon fishing than watching the fish rise through water as clear as air and inspect the fly before inhaling it gently. Nervous first-timers often strike too soon, removing the fly from the fish's mouth.

WHEN TO GO

The season in Iceland varies from river to river, but generally starts at the beginning of June and ends in late August. The first two weeks of the season are

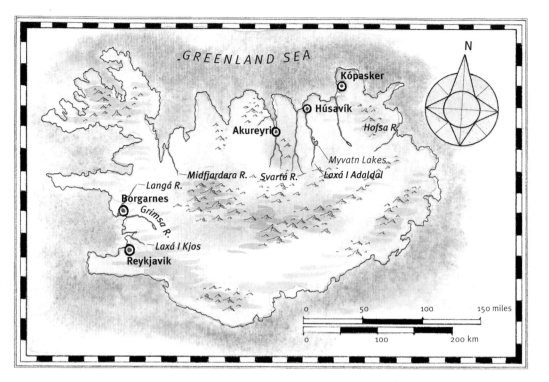

normally associated with high water levels and cold water temperatures owing to melting snow and ice from the catchment of each river. Conditions early on may require heavier sinking lines and big flies, but soon this fishing gives way to the more traditional Icelandic style of floating-line fishing with small flies.

TACKLE

RODS: Single-handed 9 ft rods for 7–9 wt lines. Double-handed 12–14 ft rods for 8–10 wt lines.

REELS: Large arbor direct-drive fly reel with capacity for 150 yards of backing plus fly line.

LINES: Predominantly floating lines, but sinking lines early in the season.

LEADERS: 8–12 lb leaders are fine on most rivers.

FLIES: Black and Red Francis, small Collie Dog tubes, Hairy Mary, Blue Charm, Stoat's Tail, Munroe Killer, Red Butt, Green Butt, and an assortment of micro-tubes 0.25–0.5 cm.

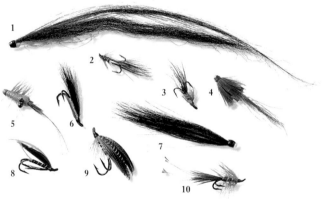

FLIES 1 *Collie Dog* 2 *Curry's Shrimp* 3 *Orange Bucktail Shrimp* 4 *Ally's Shrimp (Tube)* 5 *Green Francis (Tube)* 6 *Sheila* 7 *Sunray Shadow* 8 *Sweep* 9 *Blue Charm* 10 *Red Francis*

OPPOSITE *A salmon for dinner lies in the moist green grass of the Laxá valley.*

Prolific Eastern Margins

Russia

BILL CURRIE

"Rivers of the far north haunt you. They have an amazing numinous quality. They draw you into their atmosphere and give you a marvellous feeling of being, at last, in contact with wild tundra salmon. Ponoi has this quality. … I have at times been very aware of the serenity of the wilderness. I have fought a hard-pulling salmon while peregrines spiralled and screamed above the pool. I have waded between great rocks under the midnight sun and brought salmon in from the golden water."

Good salmon-fishing expeditions share many of the characteristics of pilgrimages. My first visit to the Ponoi had all the marks of that. It was certainly something more than a search for salmon abundance. It was an experience which drew on thirty years of waiting. When I was walking and fishing in the north of Finnish Lapland in the 1950s and '60s, I found my eyes and thoughts constantly turning to the east. From time to time I heard tales of the salmon rivers of the Kola. With a sweep of an arm and a glittering eye, travellers would say, "Over there lies the prolific eastern margin of the salmon world." It was heady stuff, but I was ready for it. I had no difficulty in believing that the Kola rivers were paradisal. There was one small practical problem, however; they were in forbidden territory. I was faced with what was in effect a war frontier between Finland and the USSR. This merely added spice to my longing to sample these Russian rivers and to see the lands of the Kola Peninsula through which they flowed. To whet my appetite, some of the rivers of the Kola tantalizingly had their headwaters in Finnish Lapland and, fishing and following them, I pressed on right to the frontier, catching large trout in pools among massive, ancient pines. Then, one day in the depths of the forest, I came across a salmon kelt (a spent fish) splashing in one of the headstreams of the Luttojoki. That river, not many kilometres downstream, crossed the frontier, took the Russian name Lotta and flowed to join the Kola River and meet the sea. Finding that solitary kelt was like meeting a messenger. It beckoned me and fermented my longing to fish for salmon in these eastern rivers of the peninsula.

Decades later, when relations between west and east had mellowed, I had the chance to go to the Kola and fish its largest river, the Ponoi. I savoured the prospects and they were compelling. The northern Kola rivers flow into what was, for me, the unknown Barents Sea – a northern and eastern ocean, salmon-rich, warmed by the tail of the Gulf Stream. The reported abundance of salmon in Ponoi was electrifying. The biologists were enthusiastic; they described important research into the salmon of this great wilderness river. Fishers who had been to the Ponoi excited me; they told me tales of salmon in plenty, wild takers, aggressive and full of wilderness spontaneity.

Ponoi is the longest of the Kola salmon rivers, over four hundred kilometres. It is also very strategically placed. It meets the sea at the most easterly point of the Kola Peninsula, where the northerly Murmanian Coast turns south and west to become the northern shores of the White Sea. The Ponoi valley divides the open, often rather stark, tundra of the northern peninsula, from the southern Kola where forests grow. There is another important difference between north and south, however. The northern rivers flow into the largely ice-free Barents Sea, while the

ABOVE *The end of a fine day's sport with good friends, a fresh fish for supper, and a helicopter ride home to the Ponoi River camp.*

rivers of the southern Kola flow to the White Sea, which freezes over in winter. Flying down from Murmansk in the helicopter – a two-and-a-half-hour journey – you get a view of the openness and heavily ice-scoured rock of the northern peninsula. It is a pre-Cambrian shield, rich in lakes, bearing only the sparsest signs of trees where valleys are sufficiently sheltered. Ponoi has cut a deep, beautiful valley into the hard rock of this shield. When you land at the camp, you will see this clearly. Well above the river, the tundra lies level and scoured; within the river valley, birch, aspen, pine, spruce and a host of Arctic wildflowers flourish. Summer migrant birds nest in the valley, falcons sweep above river pools, aquatic flies hatch and, above all, salmon in plenty run the river. In summer, Ponoi has a fecundity which can make it hard to believe that the river lies four degrees above the Arctic Circle.

The camp at Ryabaga sits among birches at the mouth of one of the smaller tributaries. A kilometre above that, the Purnache, a main feeder, joins. A short helicopter flight away the Acha flows in from the left bank. Both are memorable salmon rivers in their own right. From the Ryabaga camp, fishers cover a great swathe of excellent salmon water, embracing the two main tributaries and the wide, gliding, rich, streamy Ponoi all the way down to the estuary. Ponoi is, of course, in terms of the salmon and the delights of fishing for them, an *embarras de richesses*. For me, it always seems to be two rivers in one. The first is the panoramic Ponoi itself – a vast sweep of water hissing over the stones at Ryabaga, and two hundred and fifty metres away on the opposite bank you see the great sweep of the river gliding past cliffy red rocks and clinging birches. From the Ryabaga camp, upstream, right to the point of disappearance, the river presents a vast waterscape, punctuated in a rather theatrical way by two huge granite rocks which lie just downstream of the mouth of the Purnache. By day they glitter red; in the dusk they take on the appearance of primeval cut-outs. You look upstream to see the never-setting midnight sun. If you are fishing the Home Pool late after dinner, turn round and you will see the Ponoi above you flowing golden with its rocks and trees sombre with the darkness of silhouettes.

The second river lies at your feet as you wade. The water is tinged with peat, in summer looking like fino sherry. The streams curl round submerged stones and glide over beds of shingle, boulders and sand, forming a very active, very detailed and very fishy river. All the beats of Ponoi give you these two perspectives. On the one hand there is a vastness and on the other a detailed and intricate river within. There the river has formed a multitude of individual lies, like suite upon suite of salmon rooms, individually furnished. When I fish Ponoi I am always lifting my head to savour the panorama, then refocusing rapidly on the detail within casting distance, where my fly searches out pockets between boulders, curling streams butting off stone headlands or wide gliding sheets of water flowing over stones and sand. It is a wonderful salmon river.

BELOW *A Murmansk Munroe.*

You would expect a salmon-rich river like Ponoi to show fish constantly, but it does not. True, you do see salmon splashing here and there, but far less frequently than on Scottish rivers. I do not know why a river as full of fish as this is so secretive. The fish are no sluggards. They slash at your fly aggressively; they boil and lunge at dry and hitched flies and they are clearly enthusiastic and vigorous fish. But they do not show much. I grew to like this contrast between their covert behaviour and their sudden aggression. For example, fishing from the bank on Golden

ABOVE *A lone angler fishes the Home Pool before breakfast.*

Beach with floating line was classic summer fly-fishing – exactly what A.H.E. Wood described on the Scottish Dee in the 1930s. At one point I was casting from the rocks, a little bit above the main stream, and I could see how the long line led the fly round, touring just below the surface as the current swung it in, making the leader straighten and the fly hover. Halfway down the stream, just as Sergei, my guide, was saying that he thought I would have had a take by that point, the fly disappeared inside a sudden swirl on the water, the line tightened and a salmon was on, heaving line out as it made for the heavier stream in the middle of the river.

ABOVE *An overview of the Ponoi River camp nestled in for the night, its lights the only ones for hundreds of miles.*

166

Then it happened again, as if the second fish had learned from the first. Both were eight- or nine-pound salmon, very fresh, great fish to raise and catch. From my position a little above the water I really was in the five-guinea seats. It was visually splendid. The sweep of the line, the touring and hovering fly and the sudden boil as the salmon took were the essence of good fly-fishing. I was just beginning to feel triumphalist when my fishing companion came downstream from the little bay above. He had also taken two. I would have launched into a eulogy about the stream I had just covered, but, before I could, he pointed upstream to the bay he had just fished and said, "A perfect place."

That visit was in mid-July. The spring salmon of Ponoi had been going well since late May, but had begun to tail off by July. Rods had accounted for four

thousand fish by the end of June. These earlier fish, many between ten and twenty pounds, were followed by a run of grilse – a vast run of one-sea-winter small fish – and with them came a run of two-sea-winter summer salmon – the eight- and ten-pounders (and better) which I have described. Later in the summer the runs of large autumn salmon come into the river, fish which might be anything from ten to twenty-five pounds. If it were merely a picture of these four runs – springers, grilse, summer fish and autumn salmon – each run bringing in large numbers, that would be a very satisfying picture of a salmon river in its prime. There is, on Ponoi,

ABOVE *Skating a bomber across the current is a great way of attracting Ponoi River salmon.*

BELOW *A Crystal Willie Gunn.*

ABOVE *An American visitor about to release a fresh-run spring salmon.*

BELOW *A memento of my week on the Ponoi River – 46 salmon released and 100 rolls of film captured. What a place!*

however, another dimension. The normal order of things is that the salmon mature progressively while they are in fresh water, growing heavy with spawn which they will shed in the late autumn. On Ponoi, there is a class of fish which comes into the river in the late summer, stays in the river over the winter without spawning, stays on throughout the following summer and only then matures and spawns during the second autumn. The salmon, by that time a kelt, stays on further to over-winter in the river and it only leaves for the sea the following spring. This is a remarkable freshwater sojourn of eighteen months. It is incredible that salmon, which do not feed in fresh water, should be able to do this. What energy-packed fat and muscle they must have! This phenomenon has been clearly monitored and studied by the biological research team on Ponoi. Fish are tagged and logged and there can be no doubt that a proportion of Ponoi salmon record the longest period in fresh water known for the species.

You can fish bank, wading or boat on Ponoi. I like to have a ration of all three, but on certain beats there is some delicious fishing only to be had by using the boat. I do not just mean that the boat can take you out to cover water well beyond wading reach, to fish mid-river lies where the Ponoi curls over boulders, to long streams where the boat can let you drift down, choosing this or that angle over the water. I mean that the boat can, in a slightly contradictory way, let you fish close to the bank. The difference is that you are out fishing in, rather than in fishing out. On Clough Creek, just down from Golden Beach, and only an easy boat ride down-stream from the camp, there was a series of rocky headlands on the right bank. Glides sweep down on these and at the headland the stream breaks and, typically, forms a choppy stream below, easing off to a rippled glide over the deeper water where the headland stream has scoured out the bed. These are great places for salmon to lie. In the glides above the points you could present a steadily swinging fly coming off the lies and fish would follow and boil at it, turning and pulling and hooking themselves well as they did so. You would also find a fish – often a grilse – absolutely on the point itself, as if touching the rock point with its tail. In the broken stream and the long ripple below, you could swing or dangle the fly or make a hitched fly track over the surface as the conditions dictated. Fast streams like that were brilliant taking water. Fish would come fast to the fly, often appearing with great suddenness to take the floating-line fly or the hitch with a great surface splash followed by a hard pull.

The Ponoi guides were excellent and their knowledge of each pool was often critical. On Tomba, one of our lower beats, not far below the point at which the Tomba tributary runs in, the river slides deeply along a sheer rock face. It is the sort

of lie I might not fish at all in Scotland, thinking that the water there would be deep, possibly very deep, and salmon might well lie under rock ledges and not be interested in the fly.

Alexi, my guide, said, "Cast your fly in, right to the rock face."

I cast and plopped my #4 Claret Shrimp about eighteen inches from the mini-cliff.

"Nearer," said the guide.

I hit the water a foot off the face.

"No, no!" said Alexi. "Hit the rock with the fly!"

"You must be joking," I said. But I did it.

The biggish single hit the rock face, dropped in and was immediately taken by a good fat grilse. Yes, I did it again. In all I took four fish from this lie using Alexi's technique of bouncing the fly off the rock face. Without his advice, I would have

LEFT *Another throbbing salmon and bent rod at dusk.*

fished this pool in the conventional way, keeping off the rock to save my flies, and I would probably not have moved a single fish.

Ponoi, like all good salmon rivers, is something of a schoolmaster. It opens new doors in the mind. My salmon fishing in Scotland does not use dry fly, for the sterling reason that it does not work. I do not mean it does not work ever. From time to time a trout fisher floating a size twelve Greenwell's Glory has a kind of happy accident and finds a salmon attached. I have once or twice seen a salmon take a sea trout dap. The classic experiment carried out by G.M. La Branche at A.H.E. Wood's invitation, trying out dry fly for the prolific salmon of the Dee was, alas, resoundingly unsuccessful. Riffled hitch work in Scotland, while it moves salmon sometimes to the waking fly, is a sticky and reluctant method, and is seldom practised. In Canada, Iceland and Russia I have fished both dry and hitched flies with success. Ponoi is a place where you soon discover how good the surface fly can be – dry flies, hitched flies and those astonishing non-creatures, bombers. Surface flies on Ponoi are great sport. Some of my friends go there to fish nothing else. It is very visual, often spectacular and can be a memorable way to take salmon. On the long glide of a pool on Alexevski, where the burn flows in, salmon which were studiously ignoring the conventional fly came vigorously to a hitched fly, showing great flanks and scattering spray in great rises. On a hitched bomber on Lower Tomba I had one particular, wonderful, mental snapshot of seeing a salmon's nose appear and just sip the fly down. That two-second glimpse, and the pull which followed it, triggered a sudden burst of recognition – boyhood dapping for big sea trout in West Highland lochs and dibbling for salmon in Sutherland rivers – a powerful and deeply pleasurable cocktail, sweetness and strength and sheer excitement blended. I have to record that these very memorable Ponoi surface events have given me a problem. Dry and wet are in tension in my mind. At home, I know one of these is a false mistress, but on Ponoi I suffer from what amounts to a confliction of urges.

Salmon fishing is very much a business of hands-on at one end and remote control at the other. Everything is interpreted. The rod in your hand and the line at your fingertips perform well-rooted skills, masterful acts, ones you can practise. The fly in the water is very different. Much of the time, we can only infer what it might be doing and, as far as the reactions of the fish to the fly are concerned, we hope and trust and imagine. You become very conscious of this on a new river like the Ponoi,

especially one where salmon can be secretive. Of course, we all arrive at new waters carrying invisible baggage, preconceptions, experience of other waters. We travel to Ponoi hoping that wilderness Russian salmon will have read the right books.

I arrived with what might fairly be described as a small-fly prejudice. I fish the Scottish Dee a lot and, as spring turns into summer there, we fish small flies on a floating line. When I say small I mean size ten or twelve. To many these are trout sizes. I had heard that Ponoi salmon liked larger flies and brighter dressings, so at the beginning of my fishing I tried eights and even sixes, using conventional patterns like Garry Dog, tied with yellows and reds. The Ponoi salmon were half-hearted about these, on the whole. So, working as I say by remote control, as you might work if you had to cut a key and make it turn a lock by trial and error, I dressed a series of larger light-wire single hooks and found some of the answers I was looking for. The best pattern was a fly I have tied up for myself for years, the Claret Shrimp. It is an extremely simple fly and can be tied in one's fingers, even on the bank of the pool. It has a silver tinsel body and a long claret hair wing (I use

172

dark hairs from a wine-coloured bucktail) which I push back over the head of the fly to form long trailing fronds above and below the fly body. But the key is the tail. It is of yellow bucktail and on Ponoi I made it very long, sparse and sinuous. I used the tail to double the length of the fly. (Fishers will recognize my debt to the remarkable Ally's Shrimp in this.) The Ponoi fish slashed at this fly with its long, sinuous tail. One salmon on Tomba sprang from the water and took the fly on its downward plunge as a brown trout might do to a dropper.

We travelled widely to our beats, often by helicopter, but one of the finest pools lay right behind the camp – the Home Pool. The head was the great sheet of water upstream of our camp but the important change of pace which made the pool memorable was right behind the camp where a bar of boulders broke the flat glide and formed a long powerful rippled flow which ran for hundreds of metres, past the moored boats and down to the bend which formed the head of Golden Beach. I fished there most evenings after dinner and on one occasion, fishing in the never-ending dusk of an Arctic night, I swung through the stream a size six Garry Dog with a long golden trailing wing and I hooked a fish which ran like no other Ponoi salmon I encountered. It leapt twice in the course of one formidable run and fought with great power through several other runs and solid pulling matches. I at last brought it in, a great silver fish, bright against the dark stones at the edge of the water. I watched it kick off into the current on release. In my tent that night, I pulled out the blue card with the Atlantic Salmon Federation "Salometer" Table and read off the rather generous fact that a thirty-nine-inch salmon would probably weigh twenty-two pounds.

ASF, you are too kind. I think that fish was eighteen and a half pounds, but what the salometer cannot compute is that it was absolutely memorable.

Rivers of the far north haunt you. They have an amazing numinous quality. They draw you into their atmosphere and give you a marvellous feeling of being, at last, in contact with wild tundra salmon. Ponoi has this quality. Of course, in its abundance, it can sometimes be very upfront and over-generous in its sport. On Ponoi I have at times been very aware of the serenity of the wilderness. I have fought a hard-pulling salmon while peregrines spiralled and screamed above the pool. I have waded between great rocks under the midnight sun and brought salmon in from the golden water. Moments like these seem close to the dream I had when I peered through the Iron Curtain and longed for the chance to fish a Kola salmon river. I am glad in one way that I had to wait to make the journey. In my youth, I would have treated the visit as an expedition. When my journey to the Ponoi eventually came, it felt much more in the nature of a pilgrimage.

RUSSIA: FACTFILE

BACKGROUND

Ask anyone who has fished in Russia (especially on one of the more prolific rivers) what it was like, and the answer is almost invariably the same: "more fish than you can shake a stick at", or "fishing like it was in the good old days". Statements like these provide a pretty good summary of what Russia has come to mean in the world of Atlantic salmon fishermen.

Owing to a high number of sensitive military sites throughout the Kola Peninsula, it was as late as 1989 – the period of *glasnost* and the end of the cold war – that reports first started to trickle in about the extraordinary content of the Kola's rivers. Salmon running the peninsula's rivers from the White and Barents Seas had never come under the kind of commercial fishing pressure that other nations' stocks had had to endure. Those who had led the initial exploratory trips were reporting unheard-of numbers of fish.

The team that first fished the Ponoi River was dropped near the headwaters with rubber Avon rafts, with the intention of fishing down the river to establish some known pools and a site for a base camp. After a short time it became apparent just how many fish there were in each pool. Rather than get out of the boat and fish every pool, they decided to stop only when five salmon could be seen in the air simultaneously as they entered a pool!

With such an abundance of Atlantic salmon throughout the Kola's rivers, it is possible not only for one angler to catch several fish in a day, but also to experiment with a wide variety of techniques. There is no doubt that the Kola Peninsula rivers have few equals, a fact that is unlikely to change in the near future.

WHEN TO GO

Nearly all of Russia's Atlantic salmon rivers are north of the Arctic Circle and the season is a relatively short one. The fishing starts in June and ends in September, and as with most Atlantic salmon destinations the returning fish ascend the different rivers in varying intensities through the season. The beginning and end of the season are most noted for larger fish, and the central months of the season for the largest schools of smaller salmon and grilse.

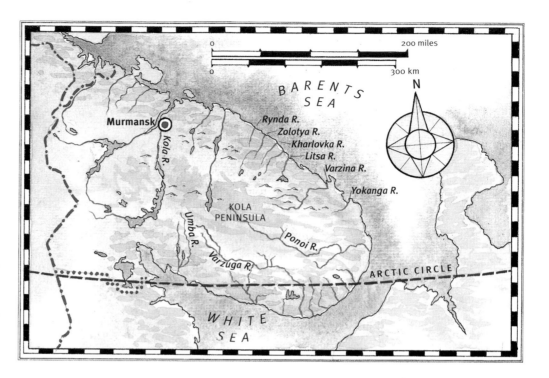

TACKLE

RODS: Single-handed rods, 9–11 ft for 7–9 wt lines. Double-handed rods, 12½–15 ft for 8–11 wt lines.

REELS: Large arbor direct-drive reels with drag systems capable of holding fly line and 150 yards of 25–30 lb backing.

LINES: A full selection of lines from floating to sinking. Most of the season will be fished with floaters and intermediates.

LEADERS: Depending on which river you fish and the size of the fish in it, 10–15 lb leader should be ample.

FLIES: Midsummer, dry flies are the most sporting: Bombers, Wulffs and Muddlers. Wet favourites are Ponoi Green, Allies and other Scottish traditional patterns.

FLIES 1 *Crystal Willie Gunn* 2 *Ponoi Red* 3 *Murmansk Munroe* 4 *Crystal Sweep* 5 *General Practitioner* 6 *Ally's Shrimp (Tube)* 7 *Garry Dog* 8 *Black & Red (Tube)* 9 *Willie Gunn (Tube)* 10 *Half & Half (Tube)*

OPPOSITE *Ponoi salmon respond aggressively to a waking bomber. In fact, some anglers prefer to use only dry flies, as it is so exciting to see the take.*

Acknowledgments

CONTRIBUTOR CREDITS

The publishers would like to thank the following authors, copyright holders and publishing houses/magazines for their kind permission to reproduce pieces in Trout and Salmon*:*

"Headwaters" by John Gierach, previously published in *Trout Bum* (Pruett Publishing, 1986), copyright © John Gierach, 1986. Reprinted by permission of Pruett Publishing Company, Boulder, Colorado.

"His Biggest Trout" by J.W. Hills, an extract from his book *A Summer on the Test* (André Deutsch, London, 1984), text copyright © André Deutsch Ltd, and Mrs S.M. May.

"Mighty Mask" by David Street, an extract from his book *Fishing in Wild Places* (Penguin Books, London, 1989), copyright © Penguin Books Ltd, and by permission of Mrs Margaret Street.

"Casting Off the Edge of the World" by Brian Clarke, an extract from his book *Trout Etcetera* (A&C Black Ltd, London, 1996), text copyright © Brian Clarke, 1996.

"The Start of the South" by Roderick Haig-Brown, an excerpt from his book *Fisherman's Winter* (Douglas & McIntyre, Vancouver, 1954), © Roderick Haig-Brown, 1959. Reproduced with permission of Douglas & McIntyre, Harold Ober Associates Inc. and Nick Lyons.

"The Dreadnaught Pool" by Zane Grey, an extract from his book *Tales of the Angler's Eldorado*, copyright © Dr Loren Grey.

"I Know a Good Place" by Clive Gammon an extract from his book *Welcome to the Chocolate Factory* (Swan Hill Press, Shrewsbury, 1990), copyright © Clive Gammon, 1990.

"Raspberries in the Rain" by Ernest Schwiebert, adapted from his book *Remembrances of Rivers Past* (The Macmillan Company, New York, 1972; Collier-Macmillan Ltd, London, 1972), text copyright © Ernest Schwiebert, 1972 and 1998.

"On Wesley's River" by Thomas McGuane, an extract from his book *Live Water* (Meadow Run Press, New Jersey, 1996), text copyright © Thomas McGuane, 1996.

"Never on Sundays" by David Profumo, text copyright © David Profumo, 1998.

"Grimsa Journal" by Nick Lyons, which first appeared in *Flyfisherman Magazine* (1975), text copyright © Nick Lyons.

"Prolific Eastern Margins" by Bill Currie, text copyright © Dr William Currie, 1998.

The publishers have made every effort to contact copyright holders. We should like to apologize for any errors or omissions, which we will endeavour to rectify in any future editions of this book.

ILLUSTRATION CREDITS

Fish illustrations on part and chapter openers are by James Prosek: those on pp.12, 28, 38, 50, 60, 74, 108, 120, 132, 146 and 162 are copyright © James Prosek, 1996, and are from his book *Trout: An Illustrated History* (Alfred A. Knopf, Inc., New York); those on pp.10, 90 and 92 are copyright © James Prosek, 1998, and were specially commissioned for *Trout and Salmon*.

SPECIAL THANKS

In addition, the publishers owe thanks to the following organizations and individuals for their invaluable assistance in the completion of this book:

Brian Fratel, Nick Armstead and Robin Elwes at Farlow's of Pall Mall; Robert Rattray at Finlayson Hughes; Henry Mountain and Tarquin Millington-Drake at Frontiers; William Daniel at Famous Fishing; Anthony Edwards; Commander Bruce Trentham; Les Kirby; Bo Ivanovic; Barry Oldham; George Ross and all at the Oykel Bridge Hotel; Captain J.R. Wilson; Duncan Watt; the Balmoral Estate Office; Peter Voy and Fraser Campbell of Assynt Estates; Peter Fowler and John Gordon of Glencalvie Estate; Stuart and Fiona Mcteare; Dennis O'Keefe; and Brian Joyce.